THE
MOON SIGN
GUIDE

The
MOON
SIGN
GUIDE

An Astrological Look
at Your Inner Life

ANNABEL GAT

Illustrations by Vesna Asanovic

CHRONICLE BOOKS
SAN FRANCISCO

This book is dedicated to my loving, generous, and beautiful mom, who always nurtured my interest in astrology and without whom this book wouldn't be possible.

Library of Congress Cataloging-in-Publication Data

Names: Gat, Annabel, author. | Asanovic, Vesna, illustrator.
Title: The Moon sign guide : an astrological look at
    your inner life / by Annabel Gat ; Illustrations by
    Vesna Asanovic.
Description: San Francisco, California : Chronicle Books, [2022]
Identifiers: LCCN 2021033468 | ISBN 9781797207094
Subjects: LCSH: Astrology. | Moon--Miscellanea.
Classification: LCC BF1723 .G38 2022 | DDC 133.5/32--dc23
LC record available at https://lccn.loc.gov/2021033468

Manufactured in China.

Design by Allison Weiner.
Illustrations by Vesna Asanovic.
Typesetting by Frank Brayton.

10 9 8 7 6 5 4 3 2 1

Chronicle Books LLC
680 Second Street
San Francisco, California 94107
www.chroniclebooks.com

Contents

Introduction

This book is your guide to one of the most magnificent and mysterious topics in astrology: your Moon sign! Yes, you don't just get a Sun sign when you are born. All of the stars and planets in the sky create a celestial snapshot of the exact moment you were born—your birth chart. The placement of the Sun and Moon, the planets, and even asteroids tells a rich story to those who study the stars.

While our Sun sign symbolizes our ego and will, and is an outward-facing part of our personality, the Moon sign represents our internal environment—our emotions, memories, and subconscious. Because the Moon sign relates to such a private side of ourselves, it is one of the most exciting to explore—all our wants and worries are touched by our Moon sign. Mystics have long associated the Moon with the mother archetype, and indeed, the Moon is like a womb; it is a metaphorical container for our feelings. Our emotions ebb and flow like the Moon, always waxing and waning. Taking time to reflect on our Moon sign provides a window into our deepest self, showing us what we need to feel secure and nurtured.

When astrologers examine the Moon in someone's birth chart, they are considering many things, including the zodiac sign the Moon is in, the house it is in, and what connections it might be making to other planets at the time of birth. This book specifically explores the first piece, the sign the Moon occupied at the time of birth. In these pages, you will learn the characteristics and personality traits related to each

Moon sign—what those who fall under that sign may need to feel comforted and secure, and how they approach and enjoy their home, family, work, friendships, and love life. Each chapter also touches on the "progressed Moon." Although this is an advanced astrological concept, I address it in this book because it provides a fascinating glimpse into how our birth charts change and grow as we do.

Not everything in this book will resonate with you, and that's OK— take what is helpful. Astrology is a beautiful tool for self-examination; however, it's hardly the final word. Astrology, after all, was created by people, and people are flawed! I certainly don't know you or your life better than you do, so please take the ideas in this book as just that: ideas for you to entertain, have conversations about, reflect on, be inspired by, or disagree with. I hope you enjoy this book and that it inspires meaningful conversations with the people you love and helps you connect deeply with your secret self, the self that is constantly evolving and reacting to new experiences and stages of life!

A Quick Overview

To start using this book, you must know what your Moon sign is, which you can figure out rather easily through online chart calculation software or an astrologer. You will need to know your birthday (day, month, and year), birth time, and birth location. If you do not have all of this data, a qualified astrologer can still help you determine your planetary placements through a process called "chart rectification," where they ask you questions about your life and when things happened to determine your birth chart.

This book has twelve chapters—one for each Moon sign—and each chapter opens with general information about the element (Fire, Earth, Air, and Water), modality (cardinal, fixed, and mutable), and planetary and tarot associations for that zodiac sign. Next, we do a deeper dive on emotions, needs, and the inner landscape. Then, we examine home and family life, a crucial aspect of the Moon sign. In this section, I discuss everything from home decor and domestic habits to childhood and parental attitudes.

We also look at career in this book. Why would we look at something so public and outward for something so private as the Moon? Well, because our Moon sign permeates everything we do, and sometimes the deepest, most private parts of ourselves drive what we do in public.

Then we examine friendship and love relationships. Although the Moon symbolizes the internal world, our interactions with others have a great deal to do with our emotional well-being. Relationships hinge on trust and security between others and ourselves. Safety, protection, and nurturance are strong themes for the Moon; for this reason, the Moon sign frequently makes an appearance when we are discussing our needs, sharing memories, and getting cozy with the people we are close to and comfortable with. It can also make a strong appearance when we are setting boundaries.

In the compatibility section, I compare the sexual and emotional chemistry between the different Moon signs. My first book, *The Astrology of Love & Sex*, explores compatibility from the perspective of Sun signs, and I could not resist doing it again, this time from the perspective of the magical, mysterious Moon. But please know: Your real-life interactions with your lover, and the level of maturity and communication you share, will always triumph over what any astrological compatibility delineation says.

While you only have one natal Moon sign, that does not mean you should only read one chapter of this book. Every chapter applies to you because all twelve zodiac signs are located in your birth chart. As you age, your Moon sign progresses through each sign, changing approximately every two and a half years. Therefore, each chapter ends with a section on the progressed Moon for that specific zodiac sign. Read each one to reveal how you have and will experience your emotional life through the lens of that sign. You can read the rest of each chapter too, as you may discover aspects about yourself that you never realized before!

If you already know your natal Moon sign, you can do a loose estimation of your progressed Moon sign by going ahead one sign on the zodiac wheel for every two and a half years of your life. Generally, your progressed Moon will be in the opposite sign when you are around fourteen and again when you are around forty, and will return to its natal placement when you are around twenty-seven and a half and again when you are around fifty-four. However, these are just estimations, and an app, a website, or a qualified astrologer who can calculate your progressed Moon's placement is the best way to go.

Now, let's get started and learn all about Moon signs!

ARIES
MOON

Aries is a cardinal Fire sign ruled by the planet Mars

Aries, a Fire sign represented by the ram, is ruled by warrior planet Mars; however, this Moon sign is less concerned with battling (though they are not afraid of a confrontation) than they are with the victory party. This Moon sign celebrates life and approaches each day with enthusiasm, optimism, and courage. Perhaps they aren't too bothered by battles because they know they will win them. Even if things do not turn out the way they plan, Aries Moon has an intrepidness about them; where what some people might call a failure, they call the beginning of a new adventure. The Moon is a symbol of comfort, and Aries Moon finds safety in taking action. Aries is a cardinal sign, making them a leader and an initiator. Like their element Fire, they light up any room they enter, but they are not ones to toy with, emotionally or otherwise!

Being the first sign of the zodiac, Aries is often called "the infant of the zodiac," and indeed, while this Mars-ruled sign is tough in many ways, Aries Moon has a deep sensitivity and vulnerability. This does not negate their fearlessness or strength. While an infant screams fiercely for comfort, it also accepts that comfort wholeheartedly and without question. Likewise, Aries Moon can be defensive, even aggressive, but they are also sensitive and have a big, open heart that generously gives, and gratefully accepts, love in all forms.

Associated with the Emperor card in the tarot, Aries has a unique discipline, strength, and sense of invincibility. There is a toughness to Aries Moon—they will not accept being wronged, and they certainly will not tolerate having to be a follower rather than the leader that they are. They have an emotional fortitude, supported by their structured approach to life, that might not be obvious to the outside observer, who may only notice their impatience and rambunctiousness. Aries Moon is decisive. They know how they feel, and they know what they want. They will get it, or if they don't, find a way to make the best of things. New opportunities are everywhere.

Going Deeper

Aries Moon is highly physical; they do not feel like themself if they have not gone for a run or to the gym. Even an Aries Moon who doesn't identify as athletic feels their best after getting their heart pumping. Whether it's blasting some music and dancing or playing recreational sports, regular exercise provides great physical and emotional benefits for Aries Moon. Plus, Aries Moon can be competitive, so playing sports is a fun way for them to channel that energy, as well as work up a sweat.

Aries is known for its me-first attitude; however, while Aries Moon can certainly have their self-centered moments, much of their preoccupation with being "first" stems from impatience and a fear of being left out or forgotten, rather than from selfishness. Eventually, they learn that pushing people out of their way to get the first slice of cake will not guarantee them a better slice and will annoy the people around them. A mature Aries Moon is patient and takes pleasure in being generous and allowing people to go ahead of them, but is also in touch with their needs and knows how to put themself first when necessary. Once Aries Moon learns their lesson about patience, life starts to feel so much more carefree, and they realize it is best to stop clenching their jaw while waiting in a slow-moving line.

Aries Moon is incredibly sincere. They aren't one for pretending to be anything other than who they are, or saying they feel a way that they don't. Such actions are so out of alignment for them that they can't keep up that sort of charade for very long. Being themself is key to feeling like themself; Aries Moon feels unsafe when they are pushed into a mode of being that is not true to who they are. They are extremely adaptable and love to take a challenge head-on, but if it requires not being authentic, they simply will not do it. They pursue their interests with passion and have great faith in themself. Aries Moon is a fighter and trusts that things will work out well—and if things don't, well, they believe there is simply more to do!

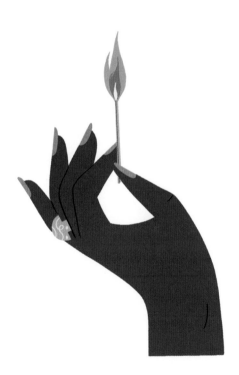

Home and Family Life

Aries Moon's home is bright and welcoming. Their ideal home features a fire keeping everyone warm and cheerful in the living room, comfortable quilts to cozy up in, and the smell of baked cookies wafting in from the kitchen. It is a pleasant scene, which might surprise someone who only knows the less domestic side of Aries Moon, the side that is always so busy doing things. Who would have guessed that Aries Moon, always excited for their next adventure out in the world, dreams of such a snug abode?

Because Aries Moon is on the go so frequently, you might think they live off of fast food and rarely make their beds (OK, perhaps this is true sometimes), but the truth is that Aries Moon prefers to live in a home that would best be described as "Grandma's cozy cabin." When it comes to their living situation, they are extremely nostalgic and want to feel enveloped by safety and comfort. Aries Moon does well in the country or in the city. No matter where they live, they'll have their local hangouts where everyone knows their name; they are often very social with neighbors.

As a housemate or partner, Aries Moon is a clear communicator about chores, when and how long guests can stay over, and other rules. As much as Aries Moon loves to party and socialize, they need organization and privacy in their home, as well as a quiet space to retreat to.

No matter what decor hangs on their wall, Aries Moon will always have a secret box of memories stashed away in the closet or under a floorboard. They had one growing up, and it contained everything from love letters and bad report cards they "forgot" to give their parents to souvenirs from vacations and objects with secret, sacred histories. Aries Moon has an easy time trying new things, but can have a hard time letting go, which means many of their childhood toys are still in a box today. Growing up, their trunk of costumes for playing dress-up was filled to the brim, and as adults, they still have plenty of flashy garments in their wardrobe, and of course, plenty of athletic clothing too, for this Moon sign loves to exercise.

Intuition was a strong theme for Aries Moon's parents, which may have left an impression on Aries Moon as a child. Perhaps the parent trusted their inner voice, which empowered Aries Moon to do the same, or they may have ignored it, sending Aries Moon on a longer journey to self-confidence. As a parent, Aries Moon endeavors to be true to themself, to trust their intuition, and to lead by example when it comes to their children.

As a sibling, Aries Moon may have been quite bossy as they were growing up. However, they also greatly enjoyed "twinning" with their siblings, unless, of course, they actually had a twin. In that case, even if they enjoyed a strong bond of friendship with their siblings, Aries Moon valued independence and experimented with different styles and interests.

At Work

The Moon symbolizes internal needs, and for Aries Moon, that need is to be a winner. This clearly shines through in their professional life, even though the Moon plays such a private role in the personality. Aries Moon is a natural entrepreneur. Working for someone else is fine (especially if that someone else is iconic and groundbreaking); however, Aries Moon has their own amazing services, products, and talents they are eager to share with the world. While Aries Moon has the reputation of being impatient, they are actually very business savvy. Even if they are too busy to be hyper-organized in the rest of their life, their company's documents are always labeled, their desk stays clear, and their to-do list is regularly tackled and updated.

Aries Moon is a born leader. If an Aries Moon is your boss, they will make sure that you have the tools you need to succeed, you have been trained well, and the team has a plan for success. Aries Moon has a keen understanding of "dressing for the job they want," and if you have an Aries Moon employee, they will not only do the tasks you assign them but also take the initiative and assume roles they want for themself down the line.

Friendships

Loyalty is very important to Aries Moon. With friends, they forgive and forget easily, understand what it is like to be moody, and know that people can get busy and go awhile without calling—and that it's nothing personal. Aries Moon is loving and forgiving as long as there is loyalty, honesty, and heart in the relationship.

Sunny Aries Moon is usually easy to approach—you might not even have to, as this Moon sign may strike up a conversation with you first. However, there can also be an aloof quality about them—they can be so focused on the task at hand that they forget to look up and see what is happening around them. If you work with an Aries Moon who has not stopped to chitchat with you, don't take it too personally too soon—they just haven't noticed you yet because they are absorbed with something else. For the most part, even though they may seem detached at times, Aries Moon is warm and loves to make new friends.

Aries Moon is highly intellectual and is particularly interested in psychology and how the mind works. They love to sit with friends over coffee and talk about *why* people behave as they do. They do not shy away from conflict and will be honest about what they think— and they expect the same from their friends. Loyalty is key for Aries Moon, but so is honesty and integrity. Aries Moon can be competitive, but they admire their opponents' sportsmanship and talent, and love to surround themself with winners. It is not unusual for them to befriend people they initially considered their rival; for Aries Moon, sometimes a worthy foe can be a worthy friend!

Love and Compatibility

The Moon symbolizes safety and comfort, and Aries Moon finds theirs through independence and freedom. However, that does not mean they are not interested in relationships or do not yearn to team up with someone. Aries Moon cannot be around controlling or jealous types, as liberty is far too valuable to them, and it is insulting when someone insinuates they can't be trusted—Aries Moon, untrustworthy?! They are far too busy, too straightforward, and too self-respecting to be in a relationship where they would behave dishonestly. Aries Moon would speedily zip out of a relationship where they're not emotionally nourished, intellectually engaged, and sexually satisfied rather than pretend everything is OK. Aries Moon knows what they want, so they may enter relationships quickly—and leave them quite quickly, too, if it becomes clear that things are not working out.

Aries Moon's type is much too cool to get caught up in power struggles, envious behavior, or pettiness. They are stylish and popular, kind and graceful. Aries Moon is attracted to intellectuals, especially people who stand up for justice. Because Aries Moon loves to make the first move and is usually fearlessly forward about their feelings, people who enjoy being pursued and appreciate grand displays of affection are great matches for them. Aries Moon also craves big displays of affection, so a partner who is not afraid to exclaim their love in a showy way (like skywriting!) would be very compatible with them. Aries Moon is protective about the people they love and expects the same sort of protection in return.

Aries Moon is all about spontaneity, and while going on a dinner-and-a-movie date is fine, they are much more excited when the script gets shaken up with some surprising adventure. If you are going to do dinner and a movie, leave room for the unexpected. Aries Moon needs to have fun and their social life is extremely important to them, so they will prefer a partner who fits in with their friend group and is interested in building community. Do you need to have the same interests? Not at all. Aries Moon loves their independence, so they are happy to have their own things going on, and they adore a partner who is excited about life and passionately exploring their own interests.

Two **Aries Moons** in love will, somehow, spend all night playfully wrestling nude in bed and still have energy the next day to tackle their to-do lists. Where do they get all this energy from?! No one knows. They feed off each other, their passion for life inspires one another, and they may even feel like they have something to prove to each other. This is a dynamic coupling, their emotional needs align, and they bounce back from tiffs quickly.

Taurus Moon really knows how to slow down and enjoy life, something Aries Moon can learn, as they tend to zip through their day and forget to notice the beauty around them. Taurus Moon will treat them to delicious dinners and fun shopping trips, spoiling them with affection. Aries Moon is actually quite a mystery to Taurus Moon, but together they explore hidden desires, making their time in the bedroom especially exciting!

Aries Moon enjoys making the first move and is not the type to keep a crush waiting, much to the delight of **Gemini Moon**, who detests waiting for a phone call. Gemini Moon appreciates how Aries Moon cultivates an exciting social life, and Aries Moon loves that Gemini Moon can make any mundane experience loads of fun. Their open approach to communication bodes well for them in the bedroom, where Gemini Moon lets their partner know what they want in great detail and Aries Moon feels no shyness about their desires!

Aries Moon has a soft spot for sentimental **Cancer Moon**. While this Fire Moon sign may have a more aggressive attitude toward life than the cautious crab Moon, Aries Moon feels at home with them, and Cancer Moon adores Aries Moon's protective energy. They have differing emotional needs; Cancer Moon requires space more often than does Aries Moon, who wants to confront things right away. If they can compromise, these two will find a fun and loyal partnership. They have a strong, magnetic sexual attraction and their lovemaking is intense and romantic.

Sparks fly when two Fire Moons come together, and **Leo Moon** and Aries Moon always have a great time. Leo Moon is all about celebrating life and knows how to help Aries Moon let loose. Leo Moon is hugely creative, and with Aries Moon, they have a partner who will encourage their artistic talents and help spot opportunities for growth. These two are noisy in the bedroom!

Virgo Moon and Aries Moon both have a straightforward approach to life that they appreciate in each other; however, Aries Moon can be a touch impatient, while Virgo Moon wants things done just right, even if it takes a little extra time. These two will have to make adjustments in their relationship, but are both grateful to have someone who is not interested in playing mind games or wasting time. Aries Moon's honest approach to what they want in the bedroom inspires Virgo Moon to open up and share their desires too.

Libra is Aries opposite, but these Moon signs know how to compromise and aren't all confrontation. With **Libra Moon**, Aries Moon feels appreciated for who they are. Libra Moon adores how opinionated this Fire Moon is, and Aries Moon appreciates having someone at their side who will stick up for them—having each other's back is so crucial to Aries Moon, and Libra Moon gets it. In the bedroom, Libra Moon loves to show off for Aries Moon; their chemistry is magnetic!

We think of **Scorpio Moon** as being the deep brooder of the Moon signs; however, Aries Moon is also extremely introspective. These two Moon signs share a curiosity about how the mind and heart work and enjoy discussing psychology, philosophy, and spirituality. Experiencing how physical Aries Moon is in the bedroom is highly arousing for Scorpio Moon! Scorpio Moon admires Aries Moon's fearlessness, and Aries Moon is captivated by Scorpio Moon's allure and mysterious charm.

Aries Moon can't help falling in love with the philosopher of the zodiac, **Sagittarius Moon**, but their late-night conversations about life and love represent only one aspect of their relationship—they also party, and make love, all night. This Moon sign combination rarely gets stuck in a rut. Their love life is passionate. For these Fire Moon signs, it is that touch of drama that makes their sex life so exciting.

Like Aries Moon, **Capricorn Moon** has a desire to be the absolute best they can be. These two Moon signs greatly appreciate this about each other, and they will always cheer each other on as they meet challenges and reach goals. They have different paces in life, but if fearless Aries Moon can slow down, and if cautious Capricorn Moon can take a little risk now and then, things might work. They have tons of sexual chemistry; Capricorn Moon knows just which buttons to push to turn on Aries Moon.

Aries Moon and **Aquarius Moon** quickly become friends. Aquarius Moon loves how confident and direct Aries Moon is; it makes them feel safe and helps them open up, as they always know where they stand with this Fire sign. Aries Moon is not afraid to be themself, and Aquarius Moon loves that. Aries Moon adores the fun games and playful banter Aquarius Moon excels at. In the bedroom, their shared love of novelty finds them experimenting with new toys, positions, and fantasies.

Dreamy **Pisces Moon** is a mystery to Aries Moon, and in a relationship, Aries Moon will have to confront many things about themself they never may have considered before. With Aries Moon, Pisces Moon learns a lot about asking for what they want. Aries Moon has an openness and generosity that deeply resonates with Pisces Moon. Together, these two can lead materially and spiritually abundant lives. In the bedroom, they both have big imaginations and enjoy exploring each other's fantasies.

Progressed Moon

The zodiac ends with Pisces, and the progressed Moon in this Water sign marks a period of completion. With closure comes sorrow and sentimentality, and the imagination bubbles with "what if" questions and fantasies. Then, the progressed Moon enters fiery Aries, the first sign of the zodiac, symbolizing a new dawn, fierceness, and joy. As the progressed Moon moves through Aries, a spirit of optimism, openheartedness, and action takes over. This period brings a boost in self-assuredness and good faith—and a dash of aggression. The progressed Moon in the sign of the ram is not afraid to lock horns.

During the time our progressed Moon is in Aries, we may be confronting issues head-on and fearlessly expressing our wants and needs—there is no tiptoeing around things. We may have some exciting firsts during this period, boldly embarking on an adventure or breaking out on our own to gain some independence. Our patience may be a little thinner than usual, but our lust for life is high, and we are feeling extremely comfortable being the boss. Holding on to a grudge feels tedious, and we are striding through the world with purpose and passion.

TAURUS
MOON

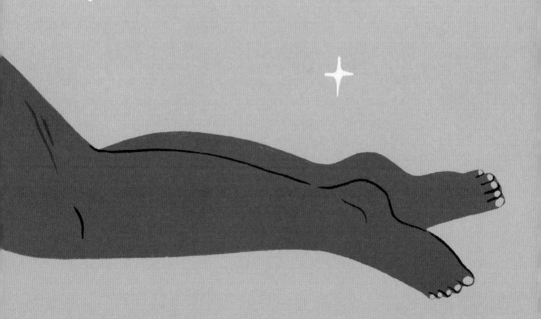

Taurus is a fixed Earth sign ruled by the planet Venus

What is the most physically comfortable place you could imagine? The most sensually pleasurable space? Imagine a massive bed of fluffy pillows and luxurious sheets, intoxicating incense wafting in the air, a box of gourmet chocolates on the nightstand, harp music playing, and a purple and pink sunset out your window. This is how the Moon feels as it moves through the sign of its exaltation, Taurus! The Moon loves to be swaddled by Taurus's grounding, secure, earthy energy. This is a placement of comfort, nourishment, fertility, and creativity. Taurus Moon displays a unique serenity and confidence. They can sometimes be slow moving or even stubborn, but they are dependable. Taurus, the bull, is not knocked down easily, and this Moon placement has a wealth of fortitude. Taurus Moon takes a determined approach to life and teaches us much about being embodied, self-possessed, and patient with ourselves.

Taurus Moon has a long memory, and while they sometimes hold a grudge, they can typically move on—they are too busy enjoying life's pleasures. They understand the importance of moderation; however, there are certain indulgences, like food and fashion, where they may lean in a little heavily. They love pleasure.

In the tarot, Taurus is associated with the Hierophant card, which is surprising being that it is such a formal-feeling card and Taurus is known to lounge around in silk pajamas. While the Hierophant's meaning is aligned with rules, hierarchy, and teaching, it also represents structure and presence, which speaks to a crucial part of Taurus's energy. Being an Earth sign (the element of physicality and form), Taurus takes a rational and material approach to things, considering the consequences and not rushing to conclusions. This languid approach provides space to digest their circumstances. Taurus is a fixed sign, and as the word suggests, Taurus Moon has an unshakable quality to them. They give themself the space they need to honor their sadness, fears, and anger, and they always make time for joy, pleasure, and gratitude. Taurus Moon trusts themself, and thus easily trust their inner voice.

Going Deeper

Taurus Moon does not need much training in how to relax. Yes, they are hard workers, but they also know when to stop checking their email. You do not have to tell them twice to go on vacation or take a longer lunch break. That said, overindulging can be an issue. Taurus Moon would be wise to examine their habits and consider how they can enjoy their favorite things in moderation—or in some cases, more consciously. Taurus Moon has a powerful rootedness that keeps them grounded while they sort through heavy emotions; however, they can also drown out their problems with distractions. When under stress, Taurus Moon would benefit from slowing down and enjoying one thing at a time rather than bombarding their senses with multiple distractions. For example, rather than eat a meal in front of the TV while texting a friend, Taurus Moon might create time for a peaceful and quiet dinner, followed by a chat with a friend, and then wrap up the evening with a film. This will give them everything they want, but in a way they can actually savor.

Everyone benefits from finding a physical activity they enjoy, and movement helps balance Taurus Moon's sometimes too-fixed energy. If they are not in the habit of working out, stretching, taking walks, or whatever physical activity they like to do, it can be hard for stubborn Taurus Moon to change their habits. Yet, once something becomes part of their routine, it is hard for them to stop—they love their rituals. They prefer to be in nature; however, a gym with luxury amenities is sure to attract any Taurus . . . they just might spend more time in the steam room than on the elliptical!

Security and finances are key themes for Taurus Moon. Building a healthy relationship to money is important, as is learning lessons around selfishness, boundaries, and hoarding resources. Taurus Moon should examine their needs around security and strive to build abundance and stability in their life—having things that are their own *and* finding the peace and openness to spread the wealth. They should share generously when it's appropriate to do so, rather than hold on to something out of stubbornness. Still, Taurus Moon needs to have the confidence, integrity, and clearheadedness to say no without feeling needlessly guilty or overwhelmed.

Home and Family Life

Taurus Moon does not do drama . . . at least, that is what you might think until you walk into their bedroom. Their home usually has a glamorous, sometimes bordering on gaudy, feel to it. Designer labels are likely to fill their closet. Each sense is accommodated—scented candles, high-tech sound systems, and gourmet groceries. Ideally, Taurus Moon would live in Versailles, so they create their own little palace wherever they might end up. The countryside is fantastic for Taurus Moon, who loves to garden; however, a city filled with good restaurants and exciting museums is also appealing.

And drama does not just translate to decor. Even though Taurus Moon is a chill individual, if you live with them, you might find them acting like royalty, refusing to share the remote control or demanding you bring them a glass of water from the kitchen. If you are having an issue with them, appeal to their love of comfort: Explain that their behavior is impeding your ability to relax, and they will have immediate sympathy for you. Security is important to Taurus Moon; while they have the patience to deal with interpersonal drama between family members or housemates, they are rattled by instability around paying bills or having broken appliances in the house.

Taurus Moon's family members may have had a theatrical or eccentric flair, and there may have been pressure to "fit in." Taurus Moon may have felt like they were shown off a lot, which would have been frustrating for them, given their down-to-earth personality. While Taurus Moon's parents may have done a wonderful job with setting standards, their vision of success may have been quite different from that of the Taurus Moon child. As an adult, Taurus Moon likely has a desire to break the norms their family set. As a parent, Taurus Moon enjoys helping their children discover their talents and express their emotions.

Learning to share is an interesting experience for Taurus Moon. As a child, they certainly figured out that marking their name on their belongings was important. It drove them bonkers when a classmate would snatch away a toy they were playing with. Your Taurus Moon sibling might have been cagey about sharing their toys (or, when you were older, their clothes); however, they likely adored caring for you, sharing an intuitive bond, and having inside jokes. As an adult, Taurus Moon is still sentimental about objects. They are tactile, and snuggling with a quilt stitched by a loved one or wearing jewelry from someone special helps them feel at home, even if they are far away from it.

At Work

Taurus Moon is not one to rock the boat, except when it comes to being in the public eye. They want to be remembered for being a maverick, a trailblazer, someone who transformed their field. Stability in their home and private life is extremely important to them, but they will take big risks in their career to achieve fame and fortune. Their dream is to be an innovator or inventor, and to be known for something groundbreaking.

In addition to being innovative, Taurus Moon is focused, detail oriented, and good at building community, so they are well suited to organizing finances, creating schedules, and coordinating projects for teams. They have a keen eye for style, so in addition to understanding the practical side of management (people and money), they often have careers that highlight their good taste and artistic talents.

If you have a Taurus Moon boss, they are someone who cares about the workplace environment (both the physical space and the relationships between colleagues). If you have a Taurus Moon employee, you have a dependable person on your team who thinks outside the box. Taurus Moon does not like to burn bridges with coworkers, and they love networking and having a vast pool of people to reach out to for professional collaborations.

Friendships

Taurus Moon can be shy at first and may need time to open up. You might share more about yourself at the beginning of your friendship; Taurus Moon is a wonderful listener, which is something they may not even realize about themself! "People just tell me things," they'll say, not realizing it's because their receptive and peaceful aura makes it so easy for people to share what is on their mind.

Your Taurus Moon friend loves a comfy night in, with takeout and a great movie: There is a laziness to Taurus energy that must be accepted if you are going to call this Moon placement your friend. But Taurus Moon also loves food and fashion, so expect them to crave nights out to show off their attire and enjoy gourmet meals, even if they don't plan wild nights of their own too frequently. Taurus Moon might spend each evening taking a bubble bath unless a friend calls with tickets to something exciting. Fortunately, Taurus Moon has an easy time connecting with active, outgoing people, and they love having friends who dream up exciting evening plans.

In friendship, Taurus Moon seeks out people who are not afraid to be bluntly honest. For example, you need to tell them if they have something stuck in their teeth—or else they will lose trust in you! When it comes to their creative endeavors, if you are not interested in seeing the painting they just finished *and* can't offer intelligent and constructive feedback, Taurus Moon is not going to consider you a close friend. Your honesty shows your integrity, which is what they need to feel safe and to trust you. Also, if you are the type of person who likes *everything*, they will be a little suspicious. Taurus Moon wants to connect with people who have taste, substance, style, and opinions.

Love and Compatibility

Taurus Moon loves romance. Taurus is ruled by Venus, the planet of love, beauty, and money, and as such, Taurus Moon is affectionate and enjoys showering others with gifts (and receiving them too!). Because security is so important to them, they can be slow to define relationships; they want to experience their lover as a responsible partner, rather than blindly trust that a commitment will work out after a whirlwind honeymoon period. They enjoy being courted, and want to be cared for, especially by brooding, mysterious types, so if you can strike a balance between domestic genius and tortured artist, they will swoon. Taurus Moon is quite cautious in their personal life, but is attracted to risk-takers and rebels. Even though they would never leave the house in a leather jacket, they are likely to bring home someone wearing one.

For Taurus Moon, falling in love is a transformative experience, which means that when they resist change, they may resist partnering. Conversely, when they crave transformation, they reach out for partnership. In an established relationship, Taurus Moon needs a partner who is committed to personal growth, or else they may feel like the energy in their life is stagnating. It's funny, Taurus Moon can be resistant to change, but is put off by people who refuse to evolve! Taurus Moon is often attracted to artists because the creative process is an inherently transformative one.

Taurus Moon has lessons to learn about sharing their possessions, which is a great thing to work out in a partnership. They are often afraid to let go of something that's theirs, and they can stress over feeling like they *must* share or risk losing their partner's affection. Through dating, they learn to overcome being possessive about partners too.

Taurus Moon is very picky, and they like to partner with someone who is too! Taurus Moon loves routine; however, because they are so selective, movie night each Thursday can't just be whatever is on television. They need to date someone with excellent taste who can curate a great date night in. Teaming up with someone who has high standards, just like they do, makes them feel like they are in a power couple of exquisite taste. While Taurus Moon is more likely to flirt with you by flashing a smile or batting their eyelashes seductively, they like to be wooed with words, so be consistent about expressing your affection verbally.

Taurus Moon picks up their pace when they fall in love with **Aries Moon**, who always seems to be in a bit of a rush. Even though Aries Moon is the straightforward type, Taurus Moon still finds them seductively mysterious, and Aries Moon greatly appreciates how reliable this Earth Moon sign is. They have a thrilling sex life: Spontaneous Aries Moon is full of surprises, and Taurus Moon will not want for novelty.

Coupling with a fellow **Taurus Moon** is a peaceful endeavor. Even if they have very different preferences (and are stubborn about them!), they both have patience, and eventually, if they love each other, their worlds will move closer together. If their relationship begins with them having the same needs and desires, it will be hard to separate these two! Their sex life is luxurious, and they take their time pleasing each other.

Gemini Moon is not particularly materialistic but is savvy enough to know that spoiling Taurus Moon with gifts will go a long way, especially after Gemini Moon may have innocently joked about something Taurus Moon didn't think was a laughing matter. They have different emotional needs, but that does not mean they can't meet halfway, and Taurus Moon can learn a lot from Gemini Moon about how to be more flexible. In their sex life, Gemini Moon's verbal approach is exciting for Taurus Moon.

It is easy for Taurus Moon to fall in love with **Cancer Moon** because they often share the same sense of humor, and Taurus Moon appreciates their intuitive approach to romance and relationships. Communication between them flows easily, and they often quickly understand each other on a body language level too. They have a passionate sex life: Cancer Moon absolutely swoons for Taurus Moon's stamina, and Taurus Moon loves how Cancer Moon makes sure all of their needs are met.

Taurus Moon feels at home with **Leo Moon**, even though they have very different approaches to their emotional lives. Taurus Moon looks sideways at dramatic, theatrical displays of emotion (unlike this Fire Moon), but they *do* enjoy decadence, which is where these two connect very easily. With communication, they can make things work, especially since their sexual chemistry is so potent! If Taurus Moon can learn the art of the grand gesture and Leo Moon can exercise some patience, this is a great (and stylish) pair.

Romance is in the air with **Virgo Moon**, as these two align in terms of emotional needs, and they always have a fun time together. Virgo Moon has a playful side that not everyone gets right away, but Taurus

Moon does! They both have very discerning taste and take pleasure in dining, shopping, and admiring art together. They greatly appreciate how reliable the other is. Their sex life is passionate and benefits from the straightforward way these two communicate.

With **Libra Moon**, Taurus Moon is challenged to break bad habits, and while these two have different emotional needs (Libra Moon wants to text a lot, while Taurus Moon prefers to nap), they are both graceful about asking for what they want and having cooperative discussions. Their sex life is full of thrills, and seduction often opens with a shopping spree for fancy lingerie and exciting toys.

When Taurus Moon falls in love with **Scorpio Moon** (Scorpio is their opposite sign), they learn valuable lessons about compromise and trust. These two have opposing emotional needs, but when they can meet halfway, a profound level of healing can take place. They will both be challenged to relinquish control . . . what a relief it will be when they each realize they have a fantastic partner they can depend on! There is an intense magnetism between them that makes their sex life electric.

With **Sagittarius Moon**, Taurus Moon is coaxed out of old patterns, which is not an easy experience for this fixed Earth Moon sign. This Fire Moon asks them deep questions that challenge the way they think about things. They have different emotional needs, but have a similar approach to pleasure (more is better), especially in the bedroom. They just need to keep their budget in mind, as they like to splurge on fancy dinners!

Capricorn Moon can sometimes be accused of forgetting how to have fun—but not with Taurus Moon, who knows how to have a good time; these two have a blast together! Plus, Taurus Moon loves the stories that worldly Capricorn Moon shares. They have similar material and emotional needs, which is a great bonus. Capricorn Moon finds Taurus Moon sexy and sensual, and Taurus Moon feels safe in Capricorn Moon's arms, making their sex life especially fulfilling.

With **Aquarius Moon**, there is plenty of wild, unexpected fun, balanced by Taurus Moon's grounded sensibility and Aquarius Moon's cool rationality. Both Taurus Moon and Aquarius Moon are fixed signs, which means once they commit to someone, they are very loyal! While they have different approaches to life (with Aquarius Moon being quite unconventional and Taurus Moon preferring to do things the tried-and-true way), there is a huge amount of sexual chemistry between them, and they continually challenge each other to keep growing.

With **Pisces Moon**, there is a fast friendship and plenty of fun, flirtatious banter. They inspire each other creatively and share a love of art and music. Both of these Moon signs love their sleep, but they sure can stay up late enjoying the magical energy of the nighttime. They just have to be careful not to encourage each other's inclination to overindulge. They enjoy sharing a social circle and can talk all day— and make love all night!

Progressed Moon

If we are not used to taking our time, we may finally slow down when the Moon progresses into Taurus. The urgency and fire of the progressed Moon in Aries transforms into grounded presence when in the fixed Earth sign of Taurus. Our desire for action morphs into a contentment with stillness. We may finally have more patience; however, we are also learning how to sit comfortably with uncomfortable feelings, and this takes time!

Having material security is of high importance. Issues like wealth and value come to the fore, but so does justice: Is it important to be fair and share our possessions, or are we allowed to have some things just for us? When should boundaries be set? How can we build mutual support with our family, friends, and community?

Beauty is also of high importance during this period. We may want to spruce up our garden and plant more flowers—why not invite loveliness into every space in our lives? We are likely to learn how to cook a great meal or two during this time, or at least find some fantastic restaurants. While the Moon progressed through Aries, we didn't think twice about eating on the go, but sitting and savoring things—not just food, but everything, really—becomes of deeper importance now.

GEMINI
MOON

Gemini is a mutable Air sign ruled by the planet Mercury

Gemini, represented by the twins, is the sign of choices, duality, and pairs. There are two sides to every coin, and Gemini covers them both. This sign has been called two-faced by some, but having eyes in the back of their head is a helpful adaptation for a Moon sign that values understanding things from each angle. Information is safety for this Moon sign. Being out of the loop equals being out in the cold for them! As information hungry as they are, logical Gemini Moon is quite a breezy, charming placement: Their inner landscape is bright, and they are full of jokes and insightful connections. They do not dwell on things for too long. Being a mutable Moon sign, Gemini is flexible and highly adaptable, always ready to consider things from a new angle. Even if they have a long-standing issue in their life, Gemini Moon knows how to step back, take a break, talk to someone new, reconnect with something old, and consider a different point of view.

Air is the element of ingenuity, connection, and communication, and Gemini Moon feels out their emotions by talking, reading, or writing about them. The Moon is a symbol of memory, and theirs is filled with recollections of the exciting discoveries they made early in life: the first time they saw a shooting star, the first scary story they heard around a campfire, the first time they felt a kiss from a crush on their cheek. Enchanted by novelty, Gemini Moon spends much of their life engaging in pursuits that can fill them with the same wonder they felt when they were young.

The tarot card associated with Gemini is the Lovers, which, on the surface, is certainly a card that speaks to partnership and communication (two themes close to Gemini Moon's heart), but on a deeper level, it speaks to duality: light and shadow, up and down, this or that, either or, both and. The Lovers observe the opposites in life and how they balance, contradict, and interact with each other. Gemini Moon has an acute awareness of duality, as they have worked through many conflicting emotions in their lives.

Going Deeper

Gemini Moon is an extremely logical individual who will seek answers for *why* they feel as they do and what to do about it. Their lesson to learn is that sometimes they need to simply stay present with an emotion rather than do something about it. When they can quiet the chatter in their mind and zero in on their feelings, a wonderful inner journey takes place. It is easy for Gemini Moon to be distracted—in some ways, this keeps them from getting too stuck in life. However, taking on too much and multitasking can become a way for them to avoid their issues. It's best for them to keep a limited amount of tasks on their to-do list, especially because they are prone to decision fatigue. Connecting with friends is high on their list of priorities: This is not a Moon sign that can stay happy for long without some gossip, flirtatious banter, or exchange of ideas.

Because they are so analytical, Gemini Moon can be an overthinker. Writing or venting to a friend is better than letting their thoughts spin in their head. Gemini Moon can greatly benefit from keeping a notepad and pen in their pocket to doodle or journal when they feel overwhelmed. Holding back from expressing what is in their heart can be poison for Gemini Moon's soul. While they love their privacy and may certainly have a secret or two, they prefer to have easy, open communication. The Moon symbolizes comfort, and they cannot find comfort if things go unsaid. Even worse is missing a message from someone or being ghosted; Gemini Moon must learn to accept that sometimes there are no answers, a hard lesson for this Air sign.

Home and Family Life

Cleanliness and organization are critical for Gemini Moon. No matter the Moon sign, most of us function best without clutter in our space, but this is doubly true for Gemini Moon, who is easily distracted. Neatly labeled boxes and orderly filing cabinets are necessary, but it is not just their belongings that they like to keep tidy; hygiene is also an important theme for Gemini Moon, who is shocked to learn that some people do not take their shoes off at the door. Keeping an organized closet is important to them. Their wardrobe is a balance of minimal pieces and fashion-forward items—they love to take part in a fad.

Social Gemini Moon loves to live in cities, where they can meet a friend at a trendy coffee shop at a moment's notice. They often get very involved with the local scene. It is rare for them to live far from a tight-knit community. As much as they love to socialize, their home often serves as a getaway from the world. On the street, they may be talking a mile a minute, but in their bedroom, covered floor to ceiling with books, it's a library, and you better shush—they are deep in thought and crave time alone to digest all the ideas and emotions that came up during the day. They are easy to get along with as a housemate or partner because they are tidy, straightforward communicators, and handy around the home, but their private space is very sacred to them, so be sure to honor that. If you travel with a Gemini Moon, they will probably pack as many books as they do changes of clothing; books make them feel at home.

Gemini Moon grew up cataloging their collection of crystals, butterflies, and seashells. They have always loved nature. As a kid, their bedsheets were covered in cartoons of their favorite animals, and their love of geography and the cosmos was reflected in the maps and posters on their walls. Gemini is the sign of the twins, and indeed, siblings (or the lack of them) often play an important role in the stories they tell of their childhood. At times, they may have struggled to outperform their sibling in sports or hobbies, but often they had a warm camaraderie and firm loyalty.

As a child, Gemini Moon was observant, copying their parents, for better or worse. Their caretakers may have had a clinical approach to raising them, doing everything by the book, or they may have been much more easygoing, creating a whimsical fantasy world for Gemini Moon to indulge in, perhaps being too lenient or distracted. Dealing with too little and sometimes too much structure growing up may have confused Gemini Moon with how to approach life. Through trial and error, they eventually find a way that works for them, and as a parent, they work hard to create a fun, structured environment for their children to explore life and feel safe.

At Work

Gemini Moon tends to gravitate toward art or media for their career, or finds themself in positions where they are tasked with coming up with catchy slogans, editing copy, or figuring out branding or marketing. Communication comes easily, which benefits them professionally. Not everyone can make cash from their creative endeavors, but Gemini Moon often finds a way! This is because they are great at networking and picking up on trends. Gemini Moon also thrives in a career in hospitality: They know how to make people feel comfortable and at home. They are savvy savers too, making them assets in nearly any sort of business.

As a boss, Gemini Moon hates to micromanage and loves to work with abstract thinkers and other creatives. If you have a Gemini Moon employee, you may find that the person you thought was a busybody scatterbrain is actually quite organized and effective. Gemini Moon may appear indecisive at times, but at work they are as sharp as a tack, do not like to waste time, and love the satisfying feeling of checking an item off their to-do list.

Friendships

Gemini Moon enjoys listening to a good story. While some friends might scroll on their phone, or even roll their eyes, when you mention your ex, Gemini Moon is an animated and invested listener, always ready to offer advice, information, and feedback. They are very witty and are sure to be one of your funniest friends.

They are very invested in their friendships, and communication is extremely important to them: Ignore your Gemini Moon friend and they will be deeply hurt. Gemini Moon may get distracted at times, but they are not the sort to flake or ghost, and they put their whole heart into connecting with others. They make friends with people quickly, and they aren't cagey or the type who keep people at bay until they pass all sorts of tests and obstacles: If you are friendly and chatty, they will be too.

Because Gemini Moon is so social, they are likely to fall into cliques from time to time, but it irritates them to feel stuck in a small, exclusive group. They do not like their social life to be limited, and they love spontaneous hangouts. Randomly running into a group of friends after a long, tiring day perks them right back up. As talkative as they may be, they are also a voracious reader with a rich internal dialogue and a passion for researching topics of interest. They often belong to a wide network of people who share their hobbies. Intellectual connection is very important to them, as they love discussing ideas. Gemini Moon is the first to join a book club, and loves having friends with whom they can discuss current events, philosophy, and politics. This is not to say that Gemini Moon can't be introverted or doesn't have introspective moments when they need quiet time to think.

Love and Compatibility

Can Gemini Moon settle down? Let's enter the mind of Gemini Moon by examining this question as they would (and, if you date a Gemini Moon, expect to parse ideas like this frequently): "Why would anyone settle? The world is constantly changing, there is so much to experience and learn. What does settling mean? Does it mean accepting that what you have right now is the best you can get? Why would you accept anything as is when there are negotiations to make, transformations to be had?" No, in that sense, Gemini Moon will not settle down; movement is what they are all about. Gemini Moon has been called fickle . . . this isn't untrue, but there is more than one side to the story. Gemini Moon might not settle down—ever!—but they certainly will pair up, often for good, so they can explore the world with a partner. Their ideal lover is someone they can trust and be best friends with. Gemini Moon adores partnership, and while they might be picky or have fleeting crushes, when they intellectually and physically connect with someone as inquisitive and intellectual as they are, they make wonderful, loyal partners.

Gemini Moon often has a companion. Since the Moon symbolizes safety and Gemini is the sign of the twins, being in a pair simply feels right to them. They adore broad-minded, well-traveled individuals. They love book-smart college types, but street-smart globetrotters are also their thing. If you have a spiritual bent to you, Gemini Moon will be intrigued. Gemini Moon is highly logical and scientific, but that is not necessarily their type. Because Gemini Moon appreciates fashion fads and trends, they are attracted to people who know what is popular. They appreciate a cohesive aesthetic: If your apartment has no vibe, your wardrobe no flare, they will be unimpressed. Good manners are a must.

Generosity is hugely attractive to them: This isn't just about showering them with gifts—which yes, please do—but they love to date someone who is nonjudgmental and can consider other people's point of view. Gemini Moon gets crushes on people who read the same books as they do, but they fall in love with folks who display kindness and an open heart toward humanity. While Gemini Moon may have many hobbies and interests, they are partial to goal-oriented individuals; someone devoted to a cause inspires them. They love studious people who also know how to have fun. If you are awkward at a party, Gemini Moon may not know what to do with you!

Friendship is such a crucial aspect of any relationship for Gemini Moon, and thankfully, it comes easily with **Aries Moon**, with whom they often share an exciting social life. The ram and twin Moons connect on a rare level, both mentally and physically. These two gas each other up, in bed and out: They both know compliments go a long way. And neither likes to wait long for a text back.

Inquisitive Gemini Moon is totally perplexed and intrigued by **Taurus Moon**, which, of course, adds to their appeal! This earthy Moon sign will teach Gemini Moon to slow down, and by doing so, Gemini Moon will discover many unknown parts of themselves. Taurus Moon adores that Gemini Moon pays attention to small details, especially the ones that make Taurus Moon feel cared for. With Taurus Moon, Gemini Moon feels safe to explore secret desires in the bedroom.

With a fellow **Gemini Moon**, everything is front and center—they are straight up with their feelings and are in constant communication about everything. They appreciate each other's flexibility, curiosity, and intellectual prowess. They are likely to have many inside jokes. They often share a busy social life as a couple. They are both very verbal in the bedroom, and their excellent communication skills keep things hot between these Air signs.

When Gemini Moon falls in love with **Cancer Moon**, they find themself exploring their intuitive abilities on a deeper level, as this watery Moon sign encourages them to get out of their head and into their feelings. Cancer Moon loves to spoil Gemini Moon, and Gemini Moon learns so much about nurturing in return. Their sexual chemistry has a sweetness, and somehow it always stays novel—both of these Moon signs have evolving needs and desires that will make for a new adventure each time they connect.

A fast friendship is formed with **Leo Moon**; this theatrical Fire sign is endlessly entertaining to Gemini Moon. These two love to party together, and while Gemini Moon is a fantastic communicator, they learn a great deal about expressing their emotions from this expressive Fire Moon sign. They have easy sexual compatibility thanks to their near effortless ability to communicate with each other, and they often send each other raunchy love notes.

Gemini Moon and **Virgo Moon** approach their emotional lives very differently. Virgo Moon can be quiet and introspective, while Gemini Moon may chatter to themself as they problem solve. However, they feel quite at home with each other, perhaps because they both love debating. Although they have different needs, their sexual chemistry is off the charts: Virgo Moon is very particular about what they like, and Gemini Moon is eager to please.

Everything clicks so easily with **Libra Moon**, a fellow Air sign. These two make a fun couple, always laughing, and align on what they need emotionally to feel safe and secure: companionship, communication, and open-mindedness. They have a busy social life and are often the couple contacted when an event needs to be planned or hosted. Libra Moon draws out the romantic side of Gemini Moon, and their sex life has a special, mutually fulfilling sweetness to it.

Brooding **Scorpio Moon** challenges Gemini Moon to break many bad habits. Gemini Moon is very adaptable, and they will frequently go through a rebirth with Scorpio Moon, a sign that is associated with transformation; if they can keep up, things can work! Scorpio Moon adores Gemini Moon's wit and storehouse of intriguing information; they will have long nights together discussing the meaning of life (and likely a bit of gossip too). Scorpio Moon's mysterious edge delights thrill-seeking Gemini Moon in the bedroom.

Sagittarius is the sign opposite Gemini on the zodiac wheel. Gemini Moon loves the idea that opposites attract, making this an exciting pairing. While **Sagittarius Moon** is an optimist who can shrug off worries, Gemini Moon is fixated on resolving issues on the spot, but they have the communication skills to compromise when conflict arises. Plus, the fire in the bedroom keeps things hot: They both love dirty talk, and Sagittarius Moon is not afraid to say exactly what is on their mind!

Capricorn Moon takes a very serious approach to life compared to playful Gemini Moon; however, this change of pace may be exactly what Gemini Moon needs. Gemini Moon approaches life with a free-spiritedness, but connecting with someone as focused as Capricorn Moon is a grounding experience. Because Capricorn Moon can be so stoic, Gemini Moon may not know what to expect between the sheets, but they'll likely discover that Capricorn Moon is just as eager to explore things in the bedroom as they are!

With **Aquarius Moon**, there is an ease and sense of adventure Gemini Moon can't find with anyone else. Aquarius Moon's freethinking, rebellious edge is a huge turn-on, and Aquarius Moon thinks no one is more hilarious than Gemini Moon. This is a couple that loves to have fun and socialize, with the party often ending in the bedroom, where they both enjoy playing with luxury vibrating gadgets and sillier novelties like edible underwear—again, they have a great sense of humor.

Gemini Moon's chemistry with **Pisces Moon** is absolutely magical. Pisces Moon's creativity is highly inspiring to Gemini Moon, and Pisces Moon feels super at home with Gemini Moon. They have different emotional needs (Pisces Moon is highly sentimental, and Gemini Moon is logical), but they are both accepting people who are willing to communicate about things. These two build incredibly sexy fantasy worlds together.

Progressed Moon

Once the progressed Moon finishes luxuriating in Taurus, it enters Gemini and starts asking questions. Material matters were the main focus while in the first Earth sign on the zodiac wheel, but it is all about intellect in this Air sign.

We are asking "why" much more as the Moon moves through this sign; we are looking for answers. Safety is found in knowledge, and comfort from books and conversation. People's motivations and opinions become especially interesting, and there is an increased desire to talk things out—communication is such a key aspect of this period. Our way of thinking about our feelings may be transformed. We may do some important written work at this time or find ourselves immersed in media. Being that this is the sign of the twins, we may find ourselves collecting two of everything.

This is an especially social time, and we may feel, on one hand, resistant to settling down, as we have so much to explore, but on the other, we may be especially keen to meet our match. Duality, of course, is a theme relating to the zodiac sign Gemini. Finding a bud, romantic or platonic, to discuss ideas, hash out feelings, and attend events with may be a priority.

CANCER
MOON

Cancer is a cardinal Water sign ruled by the Moon

Scuttling side to side navigating the tides of emotion, the crab is the first Water Sign on the wheel. From an elemental perspective, Water symbolizes emotion and flux, and Earth symbolizes physicality and stability. The shore, at the edge of land and water, is a magical place; this is the crab's home. This sway between solid and fluid, reason and creativity, quiet reflection and exuberance, is the rhythm of Cancer, a Water sign ruled by the ever-changing Moon.

Have you ever been knocked over by a wave at the beach? It is a rough fall, but you get back up. So does the resilient crab. The crab's shell is made of movable plates, not rigid walls. Like armor, the shell protects but allows mobility. The tarot card associated with Cancer is the Chariot, an armored vehicle—a symbol of strength, mobility, and spiritual ascension. Cancer Moon's emotional strength is not developed by hardness or impermeability but by flexibility and resilience.

The Moon symbolizes safety, and Cancer Moon finds comfort at home. A picture of domesticity is often painted when describing the Moon in Cancer: a cozy home that smells like cookies and drawers filled with family heirlooms. But to reduce their penchant for homemaking as a love for twee recipe books disregards the reality that Cancer Moon's metaphorical cast-iron skillet has been seasoned by a millennium's memory of feeding, caretaking, and protecting. Nurturance is the core of their being.

Emotionality and protection are major themes for Cancer Moon, but they aren't always journaling in their reading nook, or making stews in the kitchen; there's a highly artistic and expressive, outgoing side to this shy sign too. They are also entertainers, with a special sense of humor one might describe as zany. They are artists, they are lovers, and they are moody. The Moon might be happy in Cancer, but Cancer Moon is not always cheerful. However, they recognize that feelings come and go, like the tides of the sea and the waves on the shore.

Going Deeper

Moody Cancer Moon needs a wide variety of support in their daily life. Just because this sign is the domicile of the Moon does not mean that Cancer Moon has everything they need emotionally. This natural caretaker is a wonderful provider, and it may seem like they have it all worked out; however, Cancer Moon may have a difficult time making requests, so it's important to ask them what they need.

For Cancer Moon, connecting with their element is key, whether it's through days at the beach with friends or evenings alone in the tub. Visiting people and places from their past—elders in their family, ancestral lands—and connecting with their roots are also critical Cancer Moon activities. The security-conscious Moon is very comfortable in nurturing Cancer; still, Cancer Moon occasionally needs to get out of their comfort zone to be at their happiest. This means taking a leap to ask for what will make them happy, even if they feel shy doing so. Learning to make demands, negotiate, and *accept* with gratitude and without guilt are important lessons for them.

Cancer Moon loves meals. Yes, food is wonderful, but it's not just about that. Buying the ingredients at a lovely market, preparing it in their kitchen, serving it on a beautiful table, and sharing it with loved ones hits on every aspect of what brings Cancer Moon joy: creativity, nourishment, and making memories. Cancer Moon is a big fan of memories. They often romanticize the past, and the present day does not always have the same satisfying texture as experiences from long ago. Being stuck in the past has its drawbacks, and Cancer Moon can start living more in the present by honoring traditions and embracing their creative talents.

Home and Family Life

Cancer Moon is not the type to move to a new home and put off unpacking for a few weeks. They decorate their space to reflect a sense of serenity and beauty, and are often just as handy at home repair. They can pick out the wallpaper *and* put it up! They can also move to just about any environment, a busy city or quiet countryside, and make it feel like home. While they are very resourceful, Cancer Moon typically doesn't love living out of a suitcase or staying in places that lack amenities or feel incomplete.

Cancer Moon cherishes relationships in the home, whether that means living with a partner, frequently having friends occupy their guest room, or engaging with housemates or family members on a consistent basis. It's complicated: Cancer Moon also craves privacy and their own space very deeply. While they may adore living alone, being independent should not mean sacrificing support at home. In a perfect world, Cancer Moon would have both a domestic partnership to lean on for support and the space to disappear behind their bedroom door when they choose.

If you have a Cancer Moon housemate or partner, they will take the lead on creating a chore chart and will not be shy about letting you know that you missed a spot when you vacuumed the rug. But you will also live with someone who will joyfully support your goals, bake amazing pies, and give you plenty of space—because they need it too. If you're trustworthy, they might even let you borrow a piece from their wardrobe, which is usually filled with one-of-a-kind or handmade pieces—some they may have stitched together themself.

Cancer Moon's caretakers often have an intriguing past or family history and may dazzle the child with stories about their heritage; however, they may also inadvertently burden the Cancer Moon child with pressures of living up to whatever exciting history preceded them. Despite these challenges, by the time they grow up, Cancer Moon tends to be a wonderful model of emotional maturity, resilience, and creativity.

As a child, Cancer Moon paid very close attention to the relationships between family members, which gives them a keen understanding of what is needed to keep the peace and encourage connection. As a sibling, Cancer Moon can seem especially moody, setting boundaries to get their needed dose of solitude but also being a ready ear for gossip. You can always trust that your Cancer Moon sibling (or friend) will be honest with you if your outfit is unflattering—Cancer Moon is kind and cautious, with discriminating taste.

As a parent, Cancer Moon strives to create a peaceful environment. They believe that interpersonal harmony at home leads to tranquility in one's heart. It is important to them to be a fair parent, to teach the importance of sharing and community. Cancer is a zodiac sign highly associated with mothering, so with the Moon in Cancer, there is a natural inclination to be a nurturer or caretaker, and that may manifest in many ways outside of or in addition to being a parent.

At Work

While Cancer Moon doesn't dislike teamwork and does appreciate a boss they can look up to, they are generally better suited to running their own business or being an entrepreneur than answering to others. Whether they are an artist or an office manager, Cancer Moon needs plenty of autonomy. They crave the freedom and flexibility to take risks and try out new ideas. When playing games at home, winning is rarely super important to them, but it is in their career, making these shy crabs unusually competitive in the public sphere. Cancer Moon rarely acts impulsively; however, in the realm of career, they can make unexpected moves, quickly!

Cancer Moon loves to be in charge. They are caretakers at heart, so when it comes to their employees, they are deeply invested in mentoring them and being a good example. As an employee, they need respect for their work-life balance. Although home is close to every Cancer Moon's heart and working from home may be the dream, ultimately they need space between where they retreat from the world and where they hold meetings. A Cancer Moon who works from home can succeed once they figure out work-life boundaries.

Friendships

When it comes to connection, Cancer Moon is typically drawn to people who are mature, have a dry sense of humor, and are analytical thinkers. People who can handle a critique are usually Cancer Moon's oldest friends: As sweet as Cancer Moon is, they will be brutally honest with you about what they think! High achievers usually take up most of Cancer Moon's address book. While Cancer Moon is not a social climber, they do tend to gravitate toward people who are hard workers and savvy entrepreneurs.

When it comes to hobbies, Cancer Moon enjoys having friends who can share their interests in food, fashion, and finance. You can run in the same circle as a Cancer Moon for a long time without getting to know them very well, as they can be quite mysterious . . . as well as fixed about whom they sit with at the lunch table. But they are not snobby—they just like their routines, and they can be shy. Remember, they do have a hard crab shell protecting them. You can break the ice with Cancer Moon by sharing a bit of harmless gossip: They like people who are in the know and with whom they can analyze situations.

Cancer Moon's sweet and sometimes very quiet demeanor may fool you into believing they do not know how to have fun. This couldn't be further from the truth. Not only do they have an absolutely silly sense of humor, but they also love finding the most decadent, sexy, and mysterious spots. They enjoy Sunday brunch, but they also *love* midnight adventures, speakeasies, and other hidden, VIP gatherings. Cancer Moon loves home and hearth, and they might not go out each evening, but when they do, they want an experience that will *transform* them!

Love and Compatibility

Given their gravitation toward high achievers, you might expect Cancer Moon to be attracted to popular people who love the spotlight. While they love to watch their partner be applauded, it is not the person who reigned at homecoming who usually catches their eye, but the mysterious rebel in the distance, leaning against their motorcycle, contemplating something deep and important. If you look like you have a secret, Cancer Moon is likely to develop a crush on you. But, if you are aimless, they will interpret that as being passionless and will lose interest. Cancer Moon is more likely to show you their affection by baking a pie rather than writing a love letter. They are amazing poets, but when it comes to seduction, they prefer to use delicious food over flowery words. If you are taking them on a date, go somewhere intimate and private, like a dimly lit lounge.

If you are falling in love with a Cancer Moon, making memories with them is how you get them to feel the same way. Some say Cancer Moon lives in the past, but that is a misunderstanding; Cancer Moon is cautious, and they need *time* to process and contemplate their feelings. It is by reflecting on their memories that they figure things out; it's history that shows them where they stand today. Cancer Moon knows that how they feel in the moment can change. Emotions flood in and fade out, like the waves on the shore, so the past is more reliable to them. When Cancer Moon falls in love with you, it is because the impression you made has stood the test of time: They still feel goosebumps when they remember looking into your eyes, they still laugh when they remember the joke you told. It didn't all wash away the morning after.

As famous as Cancer Moon is for romanticizing the past, they usually look for a partner who values the future or wants to leave a legacy. Cancer Moon often has an interesting history, and they are seeking someone with whom they can leave a dazzling heritage. While they are remembering yesterday, they want you to mind tomorrow.

In a relationship with **Aries Moon**, Cancer Moon's cautious approach clashes with this fiery Moon's urgency; however, they are both hugely protective of each other. Things can work out if they can compromise over their different paces. Aries Moon needs to have patience when Cancer Moon has to take a time-out (this Moon sign needs their space, no matter who they are dating). They have a hugely passionate sex life: Cancer Moon knows exactly which buttons to push (acting shy and aloof, for example) to get Aries Moon going.

It is easy for Cancer Moon to fall in love with luxurious **Taurus Moon**; however, these two may never get off the couch with all the cuddling they do. Cancer Moon knows just what to feed Taurus Moon in the kitchen, and Taurus Moon knows just where to touch Cancer Moon in the bedroom. Their sexual chemistry is easy, especially since they communicate so well. They both know exactly what the other's facial expressions mean. They easily become the other's best friend.

Cancer Moon is mystified by **Gemini Moon**'s needs, but once they hammer out communication issues, they enjoy an inspiring, spiritually fulfilling relationship. While Gemini Moon regards themself as straightforward, that may not always be the case. Cancer Moon may get snappy when Gemini Moon says one thing but does another. When trust is built, these two have a powerful connection in bed;

Cancer Moon and Gemini Moon have an amazing time exploring secret desires.

When connecting with a fellow **Cancer Moon**, there is relief that they have finally met someone who intuitively understands what makes them feel safe and comfortable. The psychic connection between these two is strong. Sometimes, they might be mismatched around when they need space or closeness; however, if they can communicate their needs, they can have an incredibly strong union. Their sex life is phenomenal—they both aim to please and are in no rush to finish.

A partnership with **Leo Moon** teaches Cancer Moon much about material and financial security. Glamorous Leo Moon inspires them to achieve more in life. Cancer Moon loves being spoiled by Leo Moon. Sentimental gift exchanges between them boost their connection. But their relationship is not just about giving presents. With Leo Moon, Cancer Moon finds someone who gets their intense emotions. They both can be a bit theatrical—especially in bed!

With analytical yet amiable **Virgo Moon**, communication is easy. They are both introspective types who crave stable connection in a partnership. Their sense of humor is aligned, but they don't just joke around all day; they are both also very focused on healing, and together they can make amazing changes in their lives. Virgo Moon is sensual, and in bed, their chemistry with Cancer Moon is easy, lusty, and deep.

Libra Moon and Cancer Moon throw marvelous dinner parties; however, Libra Moon may want to stay up later chatting. Cancer Moon may be moodier than Libra Moon knows what to do with (Libra Moon feels safest with ongoing communication, but Cancer Moon can have periods of quiet reflection). Their sex life is full of fireworks. The chemistry between them is intense, and learning to please each other deepens their communication.

With mysterious **Scorpio Moon**, there is a sexy, magnetic connection. It is an easy yet thrilling union. Scorpio Moon can be intense, but Cancer Moon finds them honest and exciting, not overwhelming. Cancer Moon can have a hard time getting out of their shell, but with Scorpio Moon, they have a wild time partying and enjoying life. They are passionate lovers; both are open to whatever the other wants to try.

Curious yet cautious Cancer Moon has very different needs in a relationship than does adventurous **Sagittarius Moon**. If they can communicate, respect each other's needs (Cancer Moon's for comfort and Sagittarius Moon's for freedom), and provide a sense of safety, these two can help each other overcome emotional ruts. These two grow close through shared rituals (the more unusual and unique to them, the better). Cancer Moon appreciates Sagittarius Moon's more-is-more approach to lovemaking.

Capricorn Moon and Cancer Moon offer one another things they did not even know they needed! Capricorn Moon's solid demeanor helps Cancer Moon feel grounded in the present, and Cancer Moon offers Capricorn Moon a tenderness that melts their heart. Family and tradition mean a tremendous amount to both of them. They are opposite signs on the zodiac wheel, but they share a cautious, determined approach to life. They enjoy taking turns pursuing each other—the chase creates plenty of heat between them in the bedroom.

When falling for **Aquarius Moon**, Cancer Moon will have to make some adjustments, as these two have very different approaches to life. Aquarius Moon has an aloof demeanor that is intriguing but unfamiliar to Cancer Moon. Cancer Moon tends to cling to the past, while Aquarius Moon is forward thinking. In this relationship, Cancer Moon will have to find closure on the past before moving forward. Intimacy between these two is deep: Aquarius Moon loves to experiment, and Cancer Moon delights in trying new things in bed.

With **Pisces Moon**, there is an easy and magical connection, as they are both Water Moons that express emotion readily and are eager to explore life on a deeper level. These two make beautiful art when they are together, not to mention profound love! Pisces Moon's huge imagination inspires Cancer Moon, and they have lots of fun traveling and learning new things together. Their sex life is very emotional, and through physical touch, these two can communicate what they can't with words.

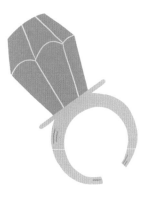

Progressed Moon

How exciting to have our progressed Moon move through the sign it rules! As it leaves chatty, social butterfly Gemini, the progressed Moon will have us turning inward as it enters Cancer, an emotional and introspective Water sign. By the time this period is over, we will have learned a great deal about how to care for and parent ourselves. We'll understand how to do more than just ride our emotions, but how to feel them deeply and not be capsized by their weight or our tears. At times, we may feel more modest than usual; however, we may also realize that our sense of humor has become splendidly absurd.

This is a powerful time for revisiting the past, processing emotions, connecting with family, and researching our ancestors. Our progressed Moon in Cancer is likely to find us nesting at home and redecorating, moving someplace better suited for us, or setting important boundaries around privacy and our sense of security. Nourishment is such a key theme of this sign: Learning to make a few delicious meals is a wonderful way to engage our progressed Moon in Cancer.

LEO
MOON

Leo is a fixed Fire sign ruled by the Sun

Does Leo Moon dream of reclining on thrones and being fed sweets by attractive attendants? Probably some of the time! But this Moon sign's inner world is not just occupied with visions of opulence and regality. Leo Moon is also massively creative, and their internal landscape is a running loop of songs they want to compose, sculptures they want to create, or poems they want to write. Performing and entertaining are some of their greatest joys.

As much as Leo Moon loves to be spoiled and adored, they have a far greater urge to create as well as to protect and maintain. They are a fixed sign and creating a life where love endures and their talents are appreciated is a high priority for them. Passionate Fire sign Leo is ruled by the Sun, and just as the Sun shines its love, Leo Moon has a special warmth and sparkle. The Moon symbolizes safety, and for Leo Moon, having fun is a core aspect of their happiness. They will find ways to celebrate life no matter what the circumstances are.

Drama is a word often associated with Leo, and while Leo Moon is theatrical, if you see them bawling at a banquet or professing their love on an airplane, do not take this as a sign of weakness or of wanting to be the center of attention. They are only human, and they know it, so they have no problem expressing the wide range of emotions that come with it. Associated with the Strength card in the tarot, Leo Moon has a deep emotional fortitude. They are not fickle or moody, and when they do feel strongly, it is deep. Like a lion roars, Leo Moon will express their feelings; hiding their emotions does not interest them.

Going Deeper

Radiant Leo Moon was born ready to entertain and party, but there is more going on with them beneath the surface. They likely have seen hardship or grief in their family or community while growing up, and therefore, creating cheer and having a good time became not just the antidote to their own sadness, but also a way to lift up other people's spirits. Entertaining the people around them and seeing the people they love smile brings them deep satisfaction. If you come across Leo Moon luxuriating in splendor, laughing with friends, and soaking in life's joy, don't assume they've never known anything but an easy life. They are grateful for what they have and are determined to create a safe, comfortable life for themself and the people they love.

In their past, Leo Moon may have struggled with fitting in, which meant putting up with frenemies, being in spaces where their talents were not nurtured, or not feeling appreciated. As they mature, Leo Moon learns how to find supportive communities where they are accepted and valued, and where their talents can help and inspire others.

Whether it's writing, painting, dancing, or cooking, creative self-expression is a crucial aspect of spiritual wellness for Leo Moon. If they were dissuaded from pursuing their creative talents when they were younger to focus on other things—or worse, if they were ridiculed or told they were not good enough—they will need to heal this wound. Discovering what they love is also crucial: If they don't make time in their busy work schedule for pursuing their passions, they may sink into sadness. Over time, some hobbies or creative pursuits may lose their meaning, but Leo Moon must remember that new passions will enter their life too.

Home and Family Life

Spend some time with cheery Leo Moon and you might expect their bedroom walls to be painted yellow, that their decor matches their good humor and fun approach to life. Yes, they probably own a karaoke machine (or at least have it on their wish list), but their home is much more dramatic, even gothic, than the sunny scene you might expect—think black wallpaper, gold accents, and woodsy incense wafting in the air. Leo Moon builds sacred spaces where they can connect with their spirituality, create art, or make love. They also enjoy campy touches—next to their meditation space might be a living room filled with kitschy objects.

Leo's generous spirit might be one reason most people don't read this zodiac sign as being particularly stubborn, but because it's a fixed sign, Leo has its rules, and for Leo Moon, having control in their home is of utmost importance. Privacy is extremely important to them, and they hate the idea that someone might look through their things or judge them for all their hair products. However, they can live happily with housemates, family, or a partner if the boundaries they set are respected. Because they are a fair ruler, Leo Moon will not expect you to wash the dishes more than they do.

Because Leo Moon loves having plenty of space and might even enjoy some nude sunbathing, they may prefer to live out in the country; however, they do enjoy the anonymity city life affords. No matter where they live, finding secret places to enjoy is one of their favorite things, whether it's a hidden waterfall or a VIP cocktail lounge tucked away on a side street. Growing up, they loved their hiding places at home and in the neighborhood. You might think that spotlight-loving Leo would never want to tuck themselves away, but it is in these private spaces that Leo Moon reconnects with their inner voice and creativity.

Their childhood rooms were often decorated with images of people they admired, folks who had gone through tremendous transformations in their life; Leo Moon was hugely inspired by people who triumphed in the face of hardship. Growing up, they likely had an adventurous fashion sense and loved wearing T-shirts bought on vacation. As an adult, they still wear plenty of clothes from their vacations, as shopping while they travel is one of their favorite things to do.

Growing up, Leo Moon may have been petty at times with their siblings and bragged a lot, but being kind, fair, and fun was still important to them. Their caretakers' relationship with money likely made a big impression on them, and as such, reflections on privilege and security entered their awareness at a young age. As a parent, they are eager to address these themes more mindfully with their own children.

At Work

Leo Moon has a deep desire for creative expression and loves performing, so they often gravitate toward the entertainment industry. Leo Moon also loves luxury and may end up in a career relating to fashion or finance.

Leo Moon is not the type to put their name on something that does not have their special touch or pass their standards, which is why group projects can sometimes stress them out (that is, until they really step into their power as a leader and teacher). They have talents they want to share, but do not want to compete with others for the opportunity to shine or risk teaming up with someone careless. They give their work their all, preferring to take their time with the creative process. As a result, they are very hands-on with any project they participate in.

They enjoy being mentors, and if you have a Leo Moon boss, you can tell they take a lot of pride in leading a team. Likewise, a Leo Moon employee can be counted on to take initiative and meet goals and expectations; they are quite competitive and enjoy winning awards and gaining recognition.

Friendships

People often joke that Leo, as a zodiac sign, needs loads of praise; however, being obsequious or fawning over them is not how to win them over. Leo Moon is very sensitive about false praise and would rather have friends who give them the harsh, honest truth when necessary. *Real* is what they are looking for in friendship and in love; they prefer people who are authentic and tell it like it is. But Leo Moon is not a downer. As a friend, Leo Moon will cheer you up on dreary days.

Decorum is extremely important to Leo Moon, and they do not last long in relationships with impolite people; however, they are often attracted to people in love and friendship who stand out in the crowd, who don't care about fitting in, and who are trendsetters themselves. A rebel who sends thank-you cards suits them well. Leo Moon enjoys having a friendship bracelet or matching tattoos; they are very loyal and love showing off how strong their relationships are.

Creative self-expression is crucial for Leo Moon's well-being, and they adore being in a social circle of artists and thinkers. They want to inspire others and be inspired. However, Leo Moon feels uncomfortable around copycats, and they will be the first to say that imitation is *not* the sincerest form of flattery. Still, Leo Moons are trendsetters and do appreciate when people incorporate their art or style into their own aesthetic (especially if people give credit to Leo Moon when it's due!).

Meaning is another critical theme for Leo Moon: Everything they do has to have heart, and their friendships must have integrity and be intellectually enriching. Like anyone, they enjoy some gossip, and they love to joke around, but they do best with people who are invested in improving themselves and making the world a better place.

Love and Compatibility

Leo Moon loves being pursued, and imagines themself sitting at the bar, batting off admirers until that one special hottie walks in, locks eyes with them, and begins wooing them as they act indifferent and ooze sex appeal. In reality, it's usually the other way around: Leo Moon loves to pursue too (like big cats do), and they are often intensely attracted to aloof cuties who are a puzzle to figure out. No matter who is doing the pursuing, *fun* is the most important part of their connection; Leo Moon loves to be around people who know how to have a good time. Leo Moon's ideal date is going someplace with plenty of music, dancing, laughter, and life. Leo Moon is all about celebration. Of course, they also love drama, so dressing up and going to dinner at a hard-to-get-into restaurant is also a great idea. Surprise weekend getaways are usually a hit with them too.

Their "type" is usually someone who has unusual hobbies or interests, who does things differently and is not concerned with fitting in; they want a partner who is unlike anyone else. They also do not want someone who fawns over them; they do not want to date a fan. Rather, they want to date a star. You might think that there isn't room for two shining lights in Leo Moon's relationship, but you couldn't be more wrong: Leo Moon wants to be with someone who dazzles.

Leo Moon needs to feel appreciated. Tell them how you feel about them, pay them compliments, run an errand for them, spend quality time with them, bring them surprise gifts, and give them plenty of cuddles and affection. If you think this is a tall order, affectionate and generous Leo Moon might not be the one for you, as they crave connection on many levels and have so much to give in exchange. They love with their whole heart and will spoil you, expecting to be adored in return. A disloyal Leo Moon is often the one to get their heart broken in the end. An inattentive Leo Moon is usually the one to end up feeling discarded. They learn in life that what goes around comes around and how you treat people matters. As such, when you are with a mature Leo Moon, they will treat you just as they expect to be treated.

Leo Moon finds **Aries Moon** intellectually stimulating, and Aries Moon is creatively inspired by Leo Moon, so these two Fire signs become close friends quickly. Aries Moon is spontaneous and will whisk Leo Moon away for unexpected weekend trips, which Leo Moon absolutely loves. They are an adventurous couple, especially in the bedroom, where these two Fire signs keep things hot all evening! Aries Moon loves Leo Moon's big imagination in the bedroom.

Taurus Moon creates an atmosphere of loving security that is deeply nourishing for Leo Moon, and Taurus Moon feels at home with this warm, generous Fire sign. However, they do have differing emotional needs: Leo Moon expresses their emotions in theatrical ways, which may take Taurus Moon some time to get used to. They have to be patient with each other. If they can do that, they can have a very successful partnership, especially with all the magnetic attraction between them in the bedroom.

Leo Moon loves sharing an exciting social life with their partner, making **Gemini Moon** a wonderful match for them. They have a powerful intellectual connection: Gemini Moon rarely has a hard time with words, but when they do, Leo Moon seems to just "get" them, which makes Gemini Moon feel validated and loved. Gemini Moon knows how to play hard to get, which drives Leo Moon wild. The chase is part of the foreplay for Leo Moon and leads to a fun time in the bedroom.

Leo Moon finds intuitive **Cancer Moon** totally enigmatic, and Cancer Moon is dazzled by Leo Moon: They have a lot of mutual admiration for each other. Leo Moon knows just how to spoil Cancer Moon, and Cancer Moon teaches Leo Moon much about spirituality and letting go. They are both sentimental and extremely romantic, and their lovemaking is often sandwiched between conversations about how much they mean to each other.

Is the world big enough for two **Leo Moons**? You might think they would be too competitive with each other; however, this is often a fantastic pairing—a power couple that inspires others while also encouraging and energizing each other. They are sunny people who enjoy having fun together. There's a deep loyalty and spiritual connection. Things are especially hot in the bedroom, which is likely covered in floor-to-ceiling mirrors, and their bed is filled with luxurious toys.

Life can be full of uncertainties, but with **Virgo Moon**, Leo Moon has a sense that everything will be OK. Feeling appreciated is major for Leo Moon, and Virgo Moon seems to know exactly what Leo Moon needs to feel loved. Leo Moon also encourages Virgo Moon to pursue their passions and release old doubts. Their sexual chemistry is highly physical, as Leo Moon gives lovemaking their all and Virgo Moon has a deep desire to please.

Libra Moon is stylish, popular, and extremely intelligent, and while Leo Moon appreciates their fashion sense, it is their wit they really fall in love with. They can talk all day (and night)! Their banter is sometimes light and sweet, but they can get into exciting debates too. They are very outgoing and have an exciting social life together. Praise is important to both of them, and their lovemaking is peppered with speeches of adoration.

Scorpio Moon has a realness about them that makes Leo Moon feel at home. Even though they have very different emotional needs (Leo Moon may party later into the evening than Scorpio Moon does), they are intensely attracted to one another. Leo Moon has a courageousness that is super sexy to Scorpio Moon, and Scorpio Moon knows how to bring some fantasy into their relationship and sex life; that's highly attractive to Leo Moon.

Leo Moon loves to party, and they have a ball celebrating life with boisterous **Sagittarius Moon**. Leo Moon loves Sagittarius Moon's optimism, rowdy sense of humor, and intense interest in the world. Sagittarius Moon adores bold Leo Moon's emotional honesty and how they give themself so fully to what, and whom, they love. These two are very compatible in the bedroom, where they slather each other in kisses and compliments.

Leo Moon and **Capricorn Moon** have a dignified air about them, but they have different emotional landscapes. There might have to be some adjustments as reserved Capricorn Moon gets used to Leo Moon belting out a song in the shower or Capricorn Moon tells jokes so dry that they fly over Leo Moon's head. But family (blood and chosen) means a great deal to both of them, and they can make a tremendous couple. Their lovemaking is decadently sensual, and their bedroom is filled with toys and lingerie.

Leo Moon wants to be with someone who stands out from the crowd, and **Aquarius Moon** does just that. They are the rebel of Leo Moon's dreams. And Leo Moon is the warm, generous star of theirs. Aquarius Moon is highly logical, and Leo Moon can be theatrical, but they often adore this about each other. Each time they make love, Leo Moon feels like they won the lottery.

On the surface, it would seem that **Pisces Moon** and Leo Moon do not have much in common, but as usual with Pisces Moon, you have to go beneath the surface. They are both extremely creative and generous; they both have massive hearts. Leo Moon is a grounding influence on Pisces Moon, and Pisces Moon inspires Leo Moon to explore hidden desires, which makes for an intensely passionate time in the bedroom.

Progressed Moon

After the Moon finishes moving through Cancer and we learn a great deal about emotional nourishment, the progressed Moon enters Fire sign Leo, and says, "I know where I belong, and I'm not going anywhere." This is a time of massive emotional resolve, confidence, and fortitude. The progressed Moon in Leo stands its ground, and everything it touches turns to gold. This is a highly creative period, and a glamorous one too. We are no longer questioning our value (or values) or our capabilities. We know who we are, what we want, and that we deserve it. This is an empowering period. It's an exciting time to share our talents with the world and simply have fun and celebrate life!

As with the progressed Moon in Cancer, there is still a strong energy around protection and nurturance, but we are eager to do it all in front of the camera instead of behind the scenes. We may star in something exciting or discover a great passion during this time. Leo is the zodiac sign that rules the heart, and while the Moon is in this sign, matters of the heart, like romance, become a big focus. This is also a time to be true to ourselves and stand up for what we believe.

VIRGO
MOON

Virgo is a mutable Earth sign ruled by the planet Mercury

Virgo Moon is down-to-earth, yet has a heavenly, ethereal quality. Ruled by Mercury, the planet of information, this is a highly cerebral Moon sign, inquisitive and introspective, though not lacking in sensuality. The Moon is a symbol of safety and security, and in Virgo, comfort comes from efficiency, order, and elegance. This observant Moon sign has always been paying attention; they have a keen understanding of how things work best. The angelic purity and meticulous fussiness associated with Virgo might have you believe they are snobby, but Virgo Moon is not stuck up, no matter how put together and accomplished they are. They have a thirst for knowledge, and even after winning accolade after accolade, they consider themself a student of their craft, always learning and improving.

Inspired by the purity found in nature, Virgo Moon brings a heavenly touch to all they do. They are organized and analytical, yet graceful, even when they are being picky. Because they are so particular, they are often seen as stubborn. It's true: Once Virgo Moon discovers the best way to do something, that is how they will do it. However, Virgo is a mutable sign, meaning it is adaptable, and Virgo Moon is open-minded about absolutely anything that *works*. This zodiac sign is all about movement and flexibility. They are accommodating, but prefer to do things in the most logical way possible.

This sign is dutiful and a helper: Virgo, the maiden, derives a deep sense of purpose from being of service to others. Virgo Moons might find themselves fantasizing about well-organized apothecary cabinets, filled to the brim with remedies they could distribute to heal the world's problems. They are in their element when they have everything in working order, are helping people, and are fixing what needs to be fixed. This is where they find comfort and joy.

The tarot card associated with Virgo is the Hermit, a card concerned with the quest for self-knowledge. This journey toward inner truth is a key aspect of the Virgo Moon experience. Virgo Moon can compartmentalize their emotions; however, if they swallow their feelings too much, they may become frustrated about why their emotions can't be tidier. Knowing their boundaries, needs, and standards creates a clearer inner environment for them.

Going Deeper

Virgo Moon can get down on themselves when they are upset about something they think shouldn't bother them; once they can accept their feelings, they will quickly digest the issue and move past it. It's one thing to be emotional about a situation and another to be upset with oneself *about* being emotional—and that is the habit Virgo Moon has to break.

Virgo Moon's routines and rituals are a grounding influence in their life. Knowing when they will see their friends and lovers, and when they can connect with their personal projects and hobbies, is crucial for a Moon sign that requires consistency and organization for their sense of security. Connecting with nature is a major source of comfort for this Moon sign, as is engaging in a spiritual practice, especially one that cultivates a sense of openness and possibility. Virgo Moon is a problem solver and healer; however, it is important that they spend just as much time helping themself as they help others—and accepting help too! Physically immersing themself in art can help calm their busy mind.

There is also a youthful quality to Virgo Moon that they would be wise to honor. Their inner child is there, eager to be entertained. Virgo Moon should step away from their hectic everyday life to play at the beach, go to a comedy show, party with friends, or do anything that inspires laughter and joy.

Home and Family Life

Virgo Moon does not care for clutter, and they need plenty of space. You will not see this Moon sign living in a tiny house, even though Virgo Moon finds this concept absolutely delightful, like something out of a fairy tale. In actuality, Virgo Moon craves spacious environments. A large living room feels grand and homey to them, and it's Virgo Moon's nightmare to have to clear someone else's clutter off their work desk, fight for room in a small bed (king size, please!), or wait in line for the restroom in their own home. Hygiene and cleanliness are, of course, close to Virgo Moon's heart. While they love a scented candle, the smell of cleaning products wafting through a sparkling kitchen is what really makes them feel comforted. Their wardrobes are sacred spaces, and their clothes aren't just for keeping them warm, or even for making them look good: To Virgo Moon, an outfit is like a talisman that magnetizes their desires. They have shoes for falling in love, a coat for important meetings, and a hat for all-around good luck. They usually prefer a tailored look.

Because Virgo Moon has a traveler's spirit, their home is neatly filled with sentimental souvenirs and trinkets from their journeys. What is a vacation destination to most is where Virgo Moon feels at home. Virgo Moon would be happy to extend their stay in a beach town, where they can retreat for quiet reflection in the winter and still party in the summer. Of course, there are some Virgo Moons who absolutely have to live in a city; having access to whatever they need, at any hour, brings them a deep sense of security. "Fitting in" in a small town is quite a bit of pressure for a Moon sign that is open to exploration and self-expression. Because Virgo Moon loves to explore, they may live in quite a few places over the course of their lives.

If you have a Virgo Moon housemate or partner, be sure to tidy up after yourself. Keeping up with the dishes or laundry will go a long way with Virgo Moon, who appreciates help with any sort of care-taking. Just do not use their beauty products without asking! This Moon sign had a thorough skin-care routine long before it became trendy. If they could have it their way, their bathroom would be a whole spa with a steam room and sauna included.

Growing up, their bedrooms were decorated with inspirational quotes and images of where and who they wanted to be. If you have a Virgo Moon sibling, they are the sort to make you pinkie swear on everything, as trust is extremely important to them. So is communication, and when it comes to their relationship with their parents, honesty and clarity are key for them. Being put in the middle of their parents, having to hide information or be the one to deliver it, is an unfair expectation of any child, and it weighs especially heavily on Virgo Moon's heart. Perfectionism is a struggle for Virgo Moon, so if they did not have parents who were encouraging of their talents, they will need to learn how to manage their own expectations and find satisfaction and pride in their work. As a parent, Virgo Moon strives to nurture their children's emotional intelligence as much as their book smarts.

At Work

Virgo Moon often shines in professions where they can share their talents around communication, marketing, and teaching. They are wordsmiths, and they delight in puns. Design also comes naturally to them, as does networking. No matter what career they have, Virgo Moon enjoys connecting people, analyzing possibilities, and formulating plans. Virgo is the sign of service, so people with this Moon placement feel a deep need to do meaningful work and help others. They enjoy teaming up, as they see its potential to double productivity, and because Virgo Moon can be a perfectionist, a partner at work means there is another person to triple-check that things are in order.

If you want to learn how to do things right, find yourself a Virgo Moon mentor. As a boss, they expect their employees to take their work seriously, and as an employee, they are reliable, consistent, and fantastic problem solvers. As focused and diligent as they may be at the office, they are also fun people to work with. Virgo Moon has a playful side and likes to let off steam as much as they like getting things done. Virgo Moon is in it for the long haul, whatever *it* may be, so they know how to pace themself to avoid burnout.

Friendships

Virgo Moon knows all the gossip, but is quite mature about keeping secrets and being discreet. Your Virgo Moon friend will always be blunt about what you need to know, but is also tactful and helpful. *Real* best describes the sort of friend this Moon placement is. They are fascinated by how things and people work, and you can easily spend hours with them dissecting everything from your circumstances to world history. While Virgo Moon highly values their independence, they also regard friends as family, always extend a helping hand, and are well known for their hospitality.

Virgo Moon is fantastic at networking and often has friends in the same or adjacent profession, so they frequently end up going into business or starting projects with their buds. Business is pleasure for this Moon sign, so you will often see them at brunches, galas, workshops, or other professional events enjoying themself! (They are not there just because their boss demanded it.) Career success is important to them, and they love connecting with people who care about it as much as they do.

If you don't meet your Virgo Moon friend through work or a community project, you might befriend them at the gym, coffee shop, or wherever else they spend their time. The Moon is all about security, and Virgo Moon is loyal to their routine, which helps keep them grounded. Once they see you at their local pub or dog run a few times, they will warm up to you, eager to discuss what's taking place in the neighborhood and beyond.

Love and Compatibility

Virgo Moon is very picky about whom they like and what sort of partnership they want to be in, and may have even attended a lecture or two on sex, intimacy, and relationships. They do not like to play games, and so are not the type to string people along. True, it might be hard to tell whether Virgo Moon is interested in you, especially after they criticize your outfit; however, if they are investing time in you, you can feel comfortable asking them where things are going. They will tell it like it is!

Virgo Moon is attracted to two main types: wandering mystics and grounded professionals. The best of both worlds is someone industrious yet spiritual, who appreciates whimsy but is also reasonable and logical. Because Virgo Moon is so dutiful and polished, you might not expect them to be attracted to free love, hippie types; however, they absolutely are. Even when they fall for the more buttoned-up business type (which they often do, as they are very attracted to busy, hardworking people), Virgo Moon will soon realize they need a partner who knows how to let loose and party. Do you have a corner office that smells like incense? If so, you will easily win the heart of Virgo Moon. They also look for generosity in a partner, not only toward them, but also toward the world. They are especially attracted to someone who is giving, charitable, and concerned about humanity's well-being.

Because Virgo Moon is so invested in whatever they do in life, you may think that they are averse to casual relationships, but this is not so. Virgo Moon delights in keeping things light and easy; in fact, they adore having a bud they can hook up with during lunch breaks or a casual lover to connect with during business trips.

As particular as Virgo Moon may be, in a long-term relationship, they are actually very flexible, valuing freedom and a productive, inter-dependent, supportive connection. When a relationship does not work out, Virgo Moon is especially hard on themself for "missing the signs," and they may overanalyze what went wrong. As they get older, though, they realize there is no scientific formula for finding the perfect relationship.

When a relationship does work, Virgo Moon is a devoted, caring partner who strives to meet their lover's needs any way they can. They want to do this relationship thing "right," which means they will engage their partner in ongoing conversations about needs and boundaries; people who are uncomfortable having discussions about details need not waste Virgo Moon's time!

In love with **Aries Moon**, Virgo Moon will learn a tremendous amount about generosity and trust. Virgo Moon feels safe when they have all the information, and with straightforward Aries Moon, they won't ever lack it. In Aries Moon, Virgo Moon finds a partner they can explore their desires with. Aries Moon will try nearly anything once, making them a fantastic partner for Virgo Moon to experiment with—in bed and out!

Chill **Taurus Moon**'s easy approach to life helps the often busy Virgo Moon relax. Taurus Moon encourages Virgo Moon to pause and enjoy life and its pleasures more deeply. These two Earth signs are all about their senses: They enjoy snuggling, massaging each other, and, of course, lovemaking. Their intellectual connection is also strong; they enjoy talking about everything from business to spirituality. The love between them is enveloping and safe, but not in a confining way—it is expansive and openhearted.

When Virgo Moon meets **Gemini Moon**, there is a deep intellectual connection. They are both the sort of people who can't rest until they have the information they need, so they will be pleased to have a partner who is always willing to discuss and analyze things. The more inside jokes they develop together, the more bonded they are. They have plenty of exciting debates, which is often foreplay for the fantastic time they have in bed.

With **Cancer Moon**, there is a fast friendship. These two Moon signs can sometimes be shy about approaching a crush, but together, there is a nearly immediate ease. They enjoy a busy social life together and can easily grow a fantastic friend circle around them. They greatly admire each other's perceptive intuition. They both require a delicate balance of time alone to think, as well as unwavering support from each other. When they make love, each time feels as thrilling as the first!

Communication is key for success with **Leo Moon**. If that can be achieved, Virgo Moon will learn things about themself they never realized before. Leo Moon is quite dramatic and open about their feelings; however, Virgo Moon sees a mysterious side to them. While Virgo Moon can be rather modest, Leo Moon sees the stylish taste-maker they are. Whole weekends can vanish when these two make love, as time doesn't seem to exist!

With a fellow **Virgo Moon**, there is a huge relief to have met someone who is comfortable being up-front about emotional needs and flexible when impasses loom. Virgo Moons find it quite sexy when their partner is in a serious mood, deep in thought, but they also share a playful approach to love, despite being so exacting in many other parts of their lives. Many seductions will begin while one has their nose buried in a book and the other finds it "just so cute!"

In love with **Libra Moon**, Virgo Moon learns a tremendous amount about what they need to feel secure and valued. Libra Moon is so refined and graceful, and Virgo Moon has such exquisite taste, that it is hard for these Moon signs to ignore each other. They share a deep need for an elegant, beautiful environment and peaceful communication. They can both be perfectionists, which bodes well for how they approach satisfying each other sexually!

Virgo Moon and **Scorpio Moon** are instant best friends thanks to their impeccable intellectual connection. They respect each other's intensity and share a passion for inner knowledge. They can be themself with each other, especially because they know the other will always be honest. They don't falsely flatter; they give each other great feedback and honest praise. Virgo Moon cannot resist Scorpio Moon's air of mystery, which makes for passionate energy in the bedroom. Scorpio Moon finds Virgo Moon's sometimes aloof approach to flirting especially cute.

When Virgo Moon is in love with **Sagittarius Moon**, a whirlwind romance may take place. Both of these Moon signs love to plan vacations and getaways, and both enjoy learning new things. They will have to adjust their paces to match each other, as Sagittarius Moon may be quicker to run off for a spontaneous adventure than Virgo Moon, who prefers to work a little longer on the itinerary. In any case, the sexual chemistry between these two is off the charts.

Virgo Moon can have a very dry sense of humor, matched only by **Capricorn Moon**, who, incidentally, is one of the funniest people Virgo Moon has ever met! They are both skeptical about many things and have a lot of responsibilities on their plates; however, they take having fun very seriously! Capricorn Moon's idea of a good time is exactly what Virgo Moon enjoys. They both have a devilishly playful side, and their bedroom behavior is exceptionally naughty.

Aquarius Moon's cool approach to life is highly seductive to Virgo Moon; however, Aquarius Moon's rebellious streak does not always match Virgo Moon's desire for simplicity and directness. This is a transformative relationship for both of them. These Moon signs may enter the relationship believing they know the right way to do things, but, with each other, they learn just how important listening and experimenting are. Neither of these Moon signs does things halfway, which makes them a happy couple in bed!

Pisces is Virgo's opposite sign, and while these Moon placements have very different needs around safety and security, they complement each other in many ways: **Pisces Moon** brings magic into the home and Virgo Moon creates a sense of organization that Pisces Moon never realized they needed! This union is one of sensitivity and awareness, and there is a magnetic pull between them. They may have different needs, but they both have the openheartedness to give each other what they want, in and out of the bedroom.

Progressed Moon

Once the progressed Moon is done showing off in Fire sign Leo, it enters modest Virgo, marking a period of introspection, where a methodical and organized search for self-knowledge takes center stage. We are interested in analyzing our emotional patterns and notice the cause and effect in our emotional world. We get back to basics, asking ourselves what feels good and what does not. There is also a return to playfulness, with a flexibility and nonchalance that are unexpected for a zodiac sign that is often considered a perfectionist.

We have increased attentiveness to healing and may even embark on an initiatory path. An interest in the esoteric may bloom, as well as in plants and nature (Virgo is an Earth sign, after all); a pet may even enter the scene! An apprenticeship may begin, or an important project may take place. Perfecting our craft is another focus. The progressed Moon in Virgo is also a key time to offer our help. We might ask, "How can I be an angel to others?" as we notice how small comforts can make a huge impact.

LIBRA
MOON

Libra is a cardinal Air sign ruled by the planet Venus

Cool and engaging, logical and sympathetic, Libra is the sign of balance, harmony, and relating to others. Scales, Libra's symbol, are tools used for objective measurement, and the desire to do the right thing is especially strong with the Moon in Libra. The Moon is a symbol for comfort, and people with this placement are at peace when things are fair; justice is a cornerstone for their sense of security. Much has been said about Libra being an indecisive sign; however, Libra is not fickle but instead concerned with making the correct choice. As an Air sign, they feel grounded in intellectual pursuits, such as listening to a passionate lecture on ethics or reading a work of literature that expands their understanding of history, human nature, and justice. Justice, naturally, is the card associated with Libra in the tarot.

When they are not engaging with exciting ideas, Libra Moon is experimenting with fashion. They have excellent taste, being ruled by Venus, the planet of beauty. But don't expect this Moon sign to be devoid of concern for the world outside their compact mirror. Libra Moon is not blind to the difficulties of life (they care about the causes they fight for dearly!), and it is very important that what they do have control over is pleasant and treated with care. Beautiful things, beautiful ideas, and beautiful connections are what lead Libra Moon to inner happiness. Their friendships and romances are crucial forms of nourishment, on par with food and water.

In a world where things are not always nice, Libra Moon seeks to make it so. They take comfort in etiquette and good manners. While some people scoff at small talk, Libra Moon sees it as an art. They love light banter, and especially love to flirt! They love ceremonies and celebrations, like birthdays and weddings. The concept of unity is comforting to them, as they are acutely pained by division and discord. Libra Moon loves any opportunity to bring people together and is happiest when decisions can be made as a group, when all sides are heard and considered.

Going Deeper

Libra Moon gives so much to others that it is critical they make time for themselves and learn how to ask for what they need. Libra is a relationship-oriented zodiac sign, but is it truly a relationship if it is one-sided giving? No! The Moon is a symbol of security, and in conscientious Libra, there is a powerful drive to accommodate; however, a happy, healthy Libra Moon should not have to compromise their own needs. Libra Moon is highly logical and verbal, so exercises like journaling or simply talking things through with a friend are very helpful for them. They may find it useful to list their needs and make plans to ensure they're met, because if they are put on the spot, Libra Moon may become indecisive or shy about making requests. As they gain more confidence communicating their needs, Libra Moon becomes a master of boundaries, in turn helping those around them set and maintain their own standards and limits.

Maintaining emotional cool is important to Libra Moon; however, they eventually realize that they are better off releasing their anger than suppressing it. Libra is the sign of balance, but if Libra Moon fools themself into believing that well-being means the scales are always still and never tremble with emotion, they will be in for a lifetime of disappointment. Emotions require constant adjustment and flexibility, so rather than approaching life cautiously and avoiding any sort of stir, Libra Moon will be stronger if they understand that feelings fluctuate.

Social connection is a key source of happiness for Libra Moon. This means belonging to a book club, maintaining a wide circle of friends, and having therapists to vent to and lovers to unwind with. While food, water, and shelter are basic needs, Libra Moon is here to remind everyone that relationships are also essential. Fashion, art, and music are also important themes in their life; they often find deep healing through the arts.

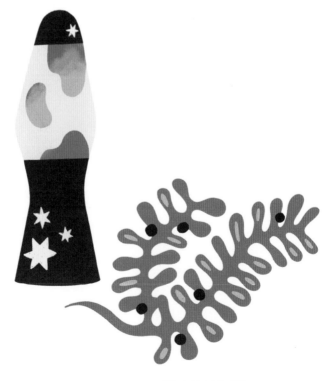

Home and Family Life

Libra Moon loves things that are time-tested, so their home decor is clean and classic; heirlooms fill their shelves, and each item is carefully chosen. Cultured Libra Moon has plenty of music and art filling their home and often has exciting guests visiting. Libra Moon enjoys living with a housemate or partner and can take the task of being a homemaker very seriously; however, they can also enjoy living alone, as it gives them freedom to entertain their many friends without considering someone else's sleep schedule. Libra is one of the most social signs in the zodiac, and with the Moon in this sign, social connection is a front-and-center need.

Because Libra Moon is so social, they tend to live in cities or busy, small towns. Libra Moon in the country is sure to maximize the space available to accommodate as many visiting friends as possible. For Libra Moon, the bedroom is as important as the home office. They have a boudoir designed with two (or more) in mind, and mood

boards abound in their workstation, which tends to be a real-life representation of the inside of their colorful, analytical, stylish mind. Their closet is filled with designer pieces, vintage finds, and sentimental hand-me-downs. They are not ones for clutter; however, it is likely they still have the shirt they wore when they were accepted to college, as this Moon sign is wistful for yesterday's outfits (even if they would not be caught wearing the same thing twice!).

Heritage, history, and tradition were prominent parts of Libra Moon's childhood; their family may have a recognizable name or a remarkable backstory, or the community they are from may be one with a long and interesting history. Societal roles were often valued and displayed by caretakers and family members, so Libra Moon was guided toward being a homemaker or provider from a young age or was expected to uphold some sort of family tradition. Libra Moon's caretakers were hard workers or often out of the home, so Libra Moon may recall feeling a duty to protect and nurture those around them.

Even though Libra is the sign of balance, Libra Moon's early life may have been quite extreme in some way, perhaps marked by arguments and disharmony, thereby filling them with a great urge to create peace in the home and community. As a child, Libra Moon was generous with their siblings and playmates, but may have taken pleasure in teasing them with witty remarks or embarrassing stories. As a parent, Libra Moon delights in passing down and beginning their own traditions. The Moon symbolizes safety, and in Libra, safety comes from interpersonal harmony, fairness, and connection.

At Work

Libra Moon often starts out life craving popularity; however, as they get older, the desire to assist and advocate for others becomes quite strong, so they might pursue a career in law or psychotherapy. They find great satisfaction and accomplishment in helping others.

Libra Moon is highly creative, but the "struggling artist" label rarely applies to them, as they are financially savvy (wonderful at raising money and managing it) and tenacious about achieving their goals. Because Libra Moon is so social, networking with others or working on a team comes easily to them.

As a boss, they take joy in nurturing their employees' talents. They love watching someone's creative abilities bloom. As an employee, they take direction easily, but they do best when given plenty of creative freedom.

As organized and tidy as Libra Moon prefers to be (they feel most comfortable in harmonious environments), their desk is likely covered in a colorful, unruly display of fabric swatches, their work space busy and bright. They prefer to keep a flexible schedule and organize projects as they choose. They enjoy working from home so they can control their environment. Their wonderful taste makes them an exquisite curator, and they are likely to be well known as an influencer. Libra is a zodiac sign that is usually ahead on trends, and Libra Moon truly feels at home when they are creatively engaging with whatever the current fad is.

Friendships

Libra Moon has a robust social life, and the people they associate with are typically glamorous. As an air sign, your Libra Moon friend is cool and charismatic, thoughtful and reasonable, and always up for a compromise. Because Libra Moon can be indecisive, they are often attracted to strong-willed people, in love and friendship. They are inspired by unwavering passion and enchanted by fiery individuals.

Libra Moon has plenty of dramatic friends who love to gossip and create a stir. However, Libra is the sign of harmony and balance, and as the Moon symbolizes safety, if they begin to feel like their friendships bring out an unfairly catty side to them, they will pull back. A lesson Libra Moon has to learn is why they are attracted to troublemakers. They are mesmerized by passionate people, but fanning the flames of drama ultimately isn't healthy for anyone. Once they mature, Libra Moons avoid these types of friendships and can be the voice of reason to their friends who need a little help being more measured or diplomatic.

Libra Moon's best and happiest friendships are with intellectuals who know how to party. They adore friends who take pride in their course of study or research, and who know where all the best happy hours are. Libra simply wants to have fun with smart people! Libra Moon loves dispensing counsel to friends, especially relationship advice. If a friend is in an argument, Libra Moon is right there to help them craft a response to their detractors. Because they are smart and stylish, they enjoy helping their friends shop and style themselves.

Love and Compatibility

Libra Moon has a very deep desire for partnership. The Moon represents safety and Libra is the sign of connection, so being in a relationship is a huge need for this Moon placement. While they value having someone to talk to and process their emotions with, they do not have a heavy approach to connection: They are light in their manner of reaching out to others. They move toward relationships with an open mind and a cheerful attitude, always eager to experiment and try new things.

Libra is one of the most flirtatious signs of the zodiac, and playful banter and romance are necessary emotional foods for them. They are likely to have many partners at once: a friend to go to concerts with, a lover for late-night rendezvous, and another pal always available to text. There may be genuine desire for a formal relationship with one (or all!) of them, or just a light, easy, flirty energy that they want to keep casual. Limiting Libra Moon from connecting with people is a sure way to put yourself at odds with them. Even when Libra Moon is ready to disconnect from a partner, doing so can be hard, as they prefer to let their lovers down easily and not hurt their feelings.

Libra Moon is romantic but unlikely to fall for mysterious, brooding types. Their sights are often set on bold, in-your-face individuals, people who are often as popular and entrenched in a scene or community as Libra Moon is, though possibly with a reputation of being rambunctious (unlike polite Libra Moon). Libra Moon longs to be wooed and courted with long-stemmed roses and love letters, but the way they imagine falling in love is frequently quite different from reality. An impromptu date someplace unexpected and exciting with someone who is direct, confident, thrilling, and leading a fast-paced life is often what makes them fall in love. "Getting along" is so important to Libra Moon that they can be conflict avoidant. This can be a good short-term plan, but long term, it can leave too many important things unsaid, so someone direct and fearless about constructive confrontation is crucial for a happy ongoing partnership.

Considerate Libra Moon is wary of confrontation, while **Aries Moon** is not afraid of a little heated debate! Libra Moon loves an intellectual debate too, but until trust can be built, there may be some frustration about why Aries Moon will not stop butting heads with them. However, Aries Moon's optimism and resilience are reassuring to Libra Moon, who adores having someone who will fight for them. Sex is great with Aries Moon, a sign that loves the chase as much as Libra Moon loves being wooed.

With **Taurus Moon**, Libra Moon may realize how important it is to let go of the past and find serenity in the present. Taurus Moon's persistence and Libra Moon's problem-solving skills can help them overcome their differences and enjoy a fantastic relationship. They have a shared love of art and beauty that bonds them. Taurus Moon brings a sensuality to the bedroom that seduces Libra Moon, and these two can experience a deep intimacy together.

Libra Moon loves exploring the world with **Gemini Moon**! They share a sharp, witty sense of humor that Libra Moon rarely finds with others. These two have loads of fun together and relate on many levels, especially emotionally. They both require plenty of verbal connection. Their sex life is full of fun, often starting with dirty talk and ending with plenty of postcoital pillow talk.

Libra Moon and **Cancer Moon** both value peace in their personal lives, but this may seem hard to achieve when Cancer Moon is being moody or when Libra Moon is too busy to pay attention to the messages Cancer Moon is trying to send. If they work on communication, they can build a beautiful home together, with Libra Moon getting the care and Cancer Moon receiving the consideration they always wanted. Their sex life is extremely passionate: Cancer Moon easily intuits Libra Moon's desires.

With **Leo Moon**, Libra Moon finds a best friend. Sometimes they can spend a whole day shopping and gossiping, but other days they may dive deeply into their shared creative projects and help each other with spiritual quandaries. When they are out and about, they are often the most fashionable couple in the room. These two are great friends, but there is nothing platonic between them in the bedroom: They probably have a mirror on their ceiling.

Virgo Moon may seem like a closed book at first—so intriguing! Eventually, Libra Moon may find that while they have different communication styles and emotional needs, Virgo Moon is actually quite generous and will open up once trust is built. They both have some insecurity issues around comfort, but together they can embark on a beautiful healing journey and have plenty of fun in the bedroom. These two will enjoy exploring their secret desires together.

A whirlwind romance is likely to take place between **Libra Moons**, even if they have a hard time deciding what to eat for dinner most nights. Fortunately, they have a wide social circle, so they can simply choose to attend whichever event they're invited to that seems the most interesting. Their needs around safety and comfort align, and they both put great effort into being kind and a good listener. In the bedroom, they are always eager to please.

Light and easy Libra Moon is entranced by brooding, sexy **Scorpio Moon**, who has a heavy energy. These two have quite different emotional needs (Libra Moon wants to talk things out; Scorpio Moon would rather sort it out in bed). However, Scorpio Moon knows just how to spoil Libra Moon, which is always a pleasure because this Moon sign loves to be doted on. Scorpio Moon teaches them much about asking for what they want, in bed and out.

Connecting with gregarious, fiery **Sagittarius Moon** feels easy for fun-loving Libra Moon. They make an exciting couple, have a busy social life, and are always in conversation, spending their days texting each other and their evenings on the couch sharing thoughts and emotions. Sagittarius Moon is a risk-taker, so they are a thrilling sexual partner for dainty Libra Moon, who will frequently blush at Sagittarius Moon's proposals!

In a relationship with **Capricorn Moon**, Libra Moon meets someone who is just as refined as they are. They have very different emotional landscapes (Libra Moon spends most of the day singing to themself while responding to social invitations, while Capricorn Moon is focused on paperwork, brows furrowed), but they have intense sexual chemistry. Capricorn's lusty energy is intoxicating to airy Libra Moon.

Both Air signs, Libra Moon and **Aquarius Moon** have an incredibly easy time relating. They both value communication and share an unmatched intellectual connection. No one entertains Libra Moon quite like Aquarius Moon can. This relationship is fun, openhearted, and supportive; they enjoy exploring each other's hobbies and blending their friend groups and communities. They have excellent sexual chemistry and find it easy to share their desires with each other.

Both **Pisces Moon** and Libra Moon believe the best in people but are wise enough to know that no one is perfect. They have different approaches to emotional life: Pisces Moon can get lost in a sea of feelings, while Libra Moon aims to be balanced. But they enjoy learning from each other; Libra Moon can help Pisces Moon approach life logically, and Pisces Moon can help Libra Moon learn even more about their intuition. Libra Moon is thrilled by Pisces Moon's sense of fantasy, especially in bed!

Progressed Moon

After the progressed Moon moves through introverted Virgo, it enters Air sign Libra, finding us eager to connect, socialize, and share ideas. Relationships are a key focus for this period; the progressed Moon in Libra teaches us valuable lessons about how other people think, feel, and experience the world. Breakthroughs take place concerning what we need in close relationships, and we learn a tremendous amount about showing up for others. This is often a glittering time in our social lives. Interest in the arts may increase, and we may discover a love for poetry or a new aesthetic. We may find ourselves swept up in a fad and excited about fashion.

The progressed Moon in Libra will find us interested in art and beauty as well as ideas about society, law, negotiation, and activism. Themes concerning justice and advocating for others are strong during this time. We are contemplating what is "fair" in our relationships, the give-and-take between ourselves and others, and boundaries and agreements. The progressed Moon in Libra seeks harmony in all things, and there is a deep emotional drive to collaborate and compromise at this time.

SCORPIO
MOON

Scorpio is a fixed Water sign ruled by the planets Mars and Pluto

The Moon is not quite sure how to cozy up with stinging Scorpio, a sign known for its passion and intensity. Scorpio is ruled by Mars, the planet of war, and also by Pluto, a planet named for the ruler of the underworld, symbolizing death and rebirth—such a contrast from the nurturing Moon! However, all this is just reflective of Scorpio Moon's complexity and mystery: They are a combination of fearless and sensitive that you don't often meet. They are highly magnetic and absolutely alluring, and are often described as mysterious.

One of the lessons the astrological Moon has to share with us, in general, is impermanence: The Moon is constantly changing shape, just like our personal situations and emotions. For this fixed Water sign, the big lessons focus on impermanence and transformation, honoring and moving past heavy and hard emotions, rather than holding a grudge or being stuck in certain patterns. Embracing the unknown is difficult for any Moon sign, but is a challenge the Scorpio Moon may be called to master.

The Moon symbolizes memory, and indeed, Scorpio Moon can get stuck in the past, replaying it from every angle. While they can hide their emotions extremely well, the coolness they project sometimes is a front for the inner torture they can experience by their intense emotions, memories, desires, and fears. Scorpio is extreme, and with the Moon in Scorpio, the inner landscape is severe, all consuming, and even smothering: The Moon is at its most feverish! Being intimately familiar with their own intense emotions, Scorpio Moons tend to be quite "psychic." They are sensitive to other people's emotions and are not easily surprised by people's behavior, partly because they are so intuitive but also because they have a deep understanding of human behavior.

Ruled by the Death card in the tarot, Scorpio is focused on transformation and rebirth. The Moon has its phases, growing from new to full, but when it is in Scorpio, the Moon cracks open and emerges anew. Deep emotional shifts happen regularly when the Moon is in Scorpio.

Going Deeper

Metaphorically speaking, the cozy, comforting Moon does not know what to do with Scorpio's knife collection. While the Moon symbolizes feeling safe and cozy, thrill seeker Scorpio's tendency to push their own limits can mean it takes a moment to realize life can be much more comfortable than they expected. The first step to nourishment for Scorpio Moon is recognizing that they might make a home in uncomfortable places. Scorpio Moon has a soft spot for haunted houses—attics filled with bats, hidden rooms, and ghosts roaming the halls; however, that does *not* mean they have to live in one, which is such a crucial lesson for Scorpio Moon to learn. Scorpio Moon can enjoy not only a phantom-free living space but also careers that don't leave them burned out and relationships that don't torture their heart (they may be shocked to learn this after having read *Romeo and Juliet* so many times). Scorpio Moon's tendency toward extremes can be worked through with some mindfulness and maturity.

Addressing the past and healing issues around control may be critical for Scorpio Moon's well-being. Scorpio Moon feels so deeply, and being a Water sign, their intensity is often expressed through their emotions. Therapies or practices that involve learning to sit with their emotions could be very beneficial. Journaling about their more overwhelming feelings, like anger, is just as important as journaling about what they are grateful for. They might feel guilty at first indulging their more difficult emotions, until they realize that repressing them is detrimental and expressing them in a healthy manner is a wonderful release. Shutting down shameful thoughts or emotions can create a stuck energy, and Scorpio Moon needs to realize that these feelings won't last forever. Practices that help them get unstuck and keep things moving are key!

Scorpio Moon benefits from steamy baths or otherwise connecting with their element, Water. Learning to cook and eat nourishing foods is a healing activity for Scorpio Moon, who may order unhealthy takeout several days in a row because they are too busy or tired. They tend to deprive themself of things that feel good, as the scorpion can be self-punishing when they feel disconnected from happiness or their creative spark, forgetting that nourishment heals. Connecting with community is key for all Moon signs; however, having a club of close confidants is crucial for Scorpio Moon, who needs to know their secrets are safe and that the bonds of friendship are unbreakable. Such friendships can help Scorpio Moon keep emotions flowing, rather than getting stuck, as holding in a secret creates a heavy weight for these sensitive Moons.

Home and Family Life

Scorpio Moon's home is often high-tech as well as environmentally friendly. They may or may not have a green thumb, but true to their sense of extremes, they may have a state-of-the-art hydroponics system or a romantic wall of ivy outside. Scorpio Moon also likes a sense of novelty and to update their decor, as they can get stuck in a rut at home if they don't keep things fresh. They love the anonymity and adventure that cities have to offer, as well as the romance of the quiet countryside. If you have a Scorpio Moon housemate or partner, you will notice that privacy is extremely important to them. They also feel most secure when shared finances are organized and paid in a timely manner.

Scorpio Moon's childhood room was likely filled with science fiction, horror, and fantasy books, toys, and posters. Scorpio Moon likes to collect; it's a healthy avenue for their obsessive side, as long as it does not drain them financially or energetically. Their childhood collection of stuffed animals or action figures was likely a source of comfort and inspiration. If you have a Scorpio Moon sibling, you likely spoke often about what life would be like when you grew up, and you probably played many games that were centered on dreams for adulthood.

As young teenagers, Scorpio Moon's fashion veered toward anything misfit that conveyed coolness and toughness: They did not want to be messed with! By the time they end their teenage years, Scorpio Moon may take on a much sweeter, preppier, or more relaxed wardrobe. Their daily leather jacket may finally be switched out occasionally for sweats, their studded belt for silk or cashmere.

Scorpio Moon's caretakers were likely remarkable in their life's journey. Lively freethinkers who were highly involved in the community, they may have been extreme or eccentric in some way, perhaps highly scientific or deeply spiritual. Scorpio Moon's caretakers may have had intense inner worlds or overcome great hardship. Coming from this background of intensity, pain, and triumph, Scorpio Moon becomes a keen observer and great detective, and they know how to keep a cool demeanor, becoming masters of displaying unbothered attitudes during the rockiest occasions. If their emotions were invalidated often, they may develop the poker face that the Scorpio archetype is well known for. In emotionally supportive homes, the Scorpio Moon child learned tremendous self-acceptance. As a parent, Scorpio Moon values heart-to-heart communication, validating their child's emotions to create an environment where they can flourish.

At Work

Scorpio Moon often feels safest working behind the scenes; however, their excellence in their career can thrust them into the spotlight, where they must contend with fame. Even though being too public may be uncomfortable for them at first, Scorpio Moon often feels they were "born" for certain achievements and may impulsively make moves toward success, which ultimately pushes them out of their shell. They easily become an expert in their field due to how committed they are to everything they do—once they find an interest, they investigate every aspect of it, fully making it their life!

Intuitive Scorpio Moon also knows what the public wants and how to give it to them; they are often very "psychic" about upcoming trends, which helps them get ahead in their careers. Financial security is important to them, but Scorpio Moon is also a generous spender, especially when it comes to investing in their professional goals. They have great intuition about where to invest their time, energy, and money.

Scorpio Moon prefers to work alone, but they can make an amazing coach and counselor. As a boss, they're great at turning potential into success and being a team leader because they're strategic about how and where to utilize a team member's skills. As an employee, Scorpio Moon needs plenty of autonomy.

Friendships

Scorpio Moon is not easy to get to know, but they are a loyal and trust-worthy friend. They also value you for the complicated person you are, not judging any difficult feelings or situations you have been through. Scorpio Moon is a pragmatic communicator, and the best way to learn more about them is to share information about yourself. If you can trust them, they will feel more comfortable trusting you . . . but go slowly! Sharing too much at once can push bonding to happen way too soon. It is important to go at a measured pace. The archetypical Scorpio famously hates "small talk," but for Scorpio Moon, not diving into the deep end right away is crucial for building trust.

They enjoy friendships where they can create collaboratively, and they like friends who can get as weird as they do. Scorpio Moon can be very straight-faced, but they love and need to get silly with their friends. While they are usually a straightforward communicator, sending non-sensical text and voice notes to their buddies is how they unwind after a stressful day. They love the absurd, and partying with their friends is an important outlet for them to let loose and forget their everyday worries. Outside their circle of close friends, they take their social life seriously, approaching it like they would their job and presenting themself in a polished, knowledgeable fashion.

Love and Compatibility

Scorpio Moon is one of the most complicated lovers in the zodiac. They believe in undying love—but may be terrified of it. They place a high value on loyalty, but will cut you off without looking back if you cross them. Between their high standards and control issues, one may wonder whether it is even possible to land a date with them. But there is another side to Scorpio Moon: playful, forgiving, almost enlightened. They are an extreme sign, so their hearts may seem sealed shut or wide open, but as they mature and feel more comfortable with flexibility in their lives, they learn to approach love and intimacy in a more balanced way.

The best way to build a lasting romance with Scorpio Moon is to get to know them slowly over time. Yes, they do jump into relationships headfirst at times, because they are thrill seekers, but you'll do better by first building a solid friendship and showing each other steadfast affection. Romance can be an escape for Scorpio, but love is also a sacred practice for them. They prefer a partner with whom they can talk about spirituality, and then snuggle and enjoy the bedroom.

Because this Moon sign may have been smothered in the past, the ideal lover gives them as much space, trust, and loyalty as possible. One thing is for sure: They are not afraid of emotional intensity! They will continually challenge themself and their loved ones to keep growing and learning.

Scorpio Moon is often attracted to slow and sensual types who carry a calming aura about them—people who smell good, with soft skin, a pleasing voice, and a luxurious fashion sense. This Moon sign is seduced by exquisite taste, and if you have an unflappable, even stubborn, energy, Scorpio Moon will be smitten. They adore someone who knows what they want and carries themself with strength. When life gets hard and it feels like things are falling apart, Scorpio Moon wants someone solid by their side.

With **Aries Moon**, Scorpio may break long-standing habits. They can get stuck in ruts, but fiery Aries Moon inspires them to be more spontaneous. They both value honesty, and while Scorpio Moon may occasionally be secretive and Aries Moon may be impatient, this partnership can work because they both fight for what they believe in. Scorpio Moon has a side that likes to play with fire, so to speak, so they find Aries Moon captivating, especially in bed!

With **Taurus Moon**, Scorpio Moon addresses their issues head-on. Interestingly, even though these two signs can be quite stubborn, they do not abandon their commitments, so they can usually come up with some amazing compromises. These two signs are opposites on the zodiac wheel, and they enjoy magnetic sexual chemistry. Taurus Moon has an ability to stay in the present that grounds Scorpio Moon, and Taurus Moon loves the sexy surprises Scorpio Moon always seems to have up their sleeve.

If sexy Scorpio Moon is looking for lovemaking that will rock their world, a night with dirty-talking **Gemini Moon** may be just what they need. If they spend more than an evening together, these two will learn a tremendous amount from each other and experience incredible transformations. They will have to adjust to each other's temperaments, but these two Moon signs enjoy learning about other perspectives. So as long as their lines of communication are open, it can work.

There is an instant connection between Scorpio Moon and **Cancer Moon**. Finally, they meet someone who is as ready to dive into intimacy as they are! Romance and creativity abound, and these two can conquer their fears together. Cancer Moon's nurturing personality makes Scorpio Moon feel safe and secure, and Scorpio Moon's wild side is loads of fun for Cancer Moon. They are devoted to each other, and this shines through in the bedroom.

With **Leo Moon**, Scorpio Moon is coy at first, but these two can create quite a cozy connection. The sexual tension between them is obvious to everyone (to Leo Moon's delight, though it might make Scorpio Moon feel a little shy). Both of these signs have a theatrical flair, but Scorpio Moon is less inclined toward public displays of affection—that's OK, since there is plenty of fire between them in the bedroom. As long as they communicate their needs and praise each other, things can work between these two sometimes stubborn Moon signs!

Communication is the key to a great relationship (and to great sex), and Scorpio Moon and **Virgo Moon** have that down. They both have a mysterious air about them, which makes for a fun and flirtatious courtship. They quickly become best friends: They have similar senses of humor and intellectual interests, and are always eager to help one another. A great amount of creativity, learning, and healing takes place when they are together.

Delicate **Libra Moon** is an enigma to Scorpio Moon, but Scorpio is the zodiac sign of the detective, so naturally, they will be excited to figure out this Moon placement. With Scorpio Moon, Libra learns big lessons about communicating their needs. Libra Moon can be almost too partner oriented and accommodating, and Scorpio Moon will not stand for this Air Moon sign being wishy-washy about their needs! Their sex life has a sacred, even spiritual feel.

Two **Scorpio Moons** feel right at home with each other—what a relief to finally meet someone who understands them, despite how complicated they are! They can handle each other's intensity and respect each other's sensitivity. Sexual intimacy is a core aspect of their union; they are absolutely magnetized by each other. Together these secretive Scorpio Moons can feel safe and understood, so they can be honest about their desires, which is not always easy for them.

Scorpio Moon adores being spoiled by **Sagittarius Moon**! This relationship teaches them a lot about self-confidence and asking for what they need, rather than assuming someone can just intuit it. There is a decisiveness about both of them, which benefits their relationship. Sagittarius Moon's generosity goes a long way with Scorpio Moon—especially in bed. Sagittarius Moon is philosophical and adores postcoital pillow talk about the universe with their mysterious Scorpio Moon.

Capricorn Moon and Scorpio Moon form a friendship quickly—there's much sympathy between these two Moon signs, both of whom tend to be guarded. They share a strong intellectual connection and emotional bond. They both value things that are old and time-tested, so family and legacy are important themes for both of them. With Capricorn Moon, Scorpio Moon has a delightful friend to be naughty with, in and out of bed!

Scorpio Moon feels like they have known **Aquarius Moon** for a lifetime (even if they just met!), yet Aquarius Moon finds Scorpio Moon a total mystery (a sexy one!). They can tell there is something exciting brewing just beneath Scorpio Moon's surface and they want to know what it is. This tension makes for an exciting sex life. They both have a powerful intensity and may have a hard time figuring out the best way to navigate emotional upsets, but with patience, these two geniuses can solve any problem.

Scorpio Moon and **Pisces Moon** have a solid friendship, which can blossom into a thrilling and emotionally fulfilling romance. They love to support and encourage each other. Water Moons are quite emotional and are grateful to have someone in their life who "gets it." Scorpio Moon's passion and intensity bolsters Pisces Moon's morale, and Pisces Moon's whimsy keeps Scorpio Moon inspired. They have exciting adventures together, especially in the bedroom!

Progressed Moon

When the Moon leaves the sign of balance, Libra, it enters the sign of extremes, Scorpio. Relationships are the major emotional focus when the Moon is in Libra. While this focus stays as the Moon progresses through feelings-oriented Water sign Scorpio, the point is less about communication and the intellectual side of partnership and more about exploring emotional depth and learning to share resources. Intimacy is a major theme during the time the progressed Moon moves through Scorpio, and deep, life-changing relationships take place.

We are also challenged to confront discomfort at home and in our personal lives. We'll need to examine any less-than-nourishing situations that we may have accepted because of an unconscious effort to heal old wounds. This is a powerful time to break cycles, engage in therapy, and bring to light patterns, or even obsessions, that require attention and healing. This is one of the most intense periods of our lives. It is an experience that will forever transform us, as Scorpio is the sign of rebirth.

SAGITTARIUS
MOON

Sagittarius is a mutable Fire sign ruled by the planet Jupiter

Sagittarius Moon is grand: Wherever they are, they stretch themselves out, their jovial aura touching everything in the room. It is hard not to feel like all will be well when you are in their presence, as they are so intelligent, confident, and optimistic. The Moon symbolizes one's inner life and memories, and for Sagittarius Moon, the internal world is filled with recollections of adventure, triumph, and growth, even after the hardest times. They are scholarly, but they also love to party. Both intellectual and physical, Sagittarius Moon is a profound examiner and robust experiencer of emotion.

Sagittarius is a Fire sign, imbuing this Moon placement with courage, creativity, and passion. The inner landscape of Sagittarius Moon is ribboned with rainbows, symbols of good luck and sunshine after rain. If riches reside at the end of these rainbows, Sagittarius Moon doesn't mind that it's impossible to ever reach them—it's all about the journey for this Moon sign. Sagittarius Moon has so much abundance within them that pots of glittering gold, while exciting, are nothing compared to the treasures of their spirit. Sagittarius is a mutable sign, and they value adaptability in themself and others. Sagittarius is ruled by Jupiter, the planet of growth, making expansiveness a key aspect of this Moon sign's sense of security.

Sagittarius's tarot card is Temperance, and while moderation and restraint are probably not what come to mind when considering this Moon sign (exuberant, spirited, or dashing would be more likely), the meaning of this card is about so much more than a balanced approach to life. This is the alchemy card and is all about combination and creation. With the right measurements, two very different things can be brought together and made into something new and wonderful. For Sagittarius Moon, life is full of possibilities, and like the Temperance card, with the right ingredients, and the right aim, this centaur archer can achieve anything.

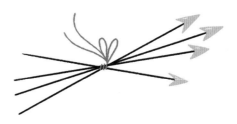

Going Deeper

You know that feeling you get when you learn something new, all the dots start to connect, and you feel limitless, like everything makes sense? Sagittarius Moon absolutely lives for that aha moment. They love novelty, not because they are bored by life and need new distractions, but because new experiences are the food that nourishes their spirit.

Sagittarius Moon often enjoys travel, and the farther away they can get, the more exciting it is. However, they need to pause occasionally and consider if their voyages are truly about gaining enriching life experiences, or about running away from something. A major moment of maturity arrives for Sagittarius Moon when they stop to ask themself if the ticket they are purchasing is for a fun vacation or an escape from their problems.

Limitlessness is one of Sagittarius Moon's favorite words, but boundaries are also crucial. They have a strong sense of justice and value doing the *right thing*. They like to play by the rules; however, Sagittarius Moon should remember that they can set their own rules too. They might spend so much time wondering what someone else's limits are that they forget to consider their own. While they are extremely generous people, picking up the check at each and every dinner out with friends may not be the wisest choice. They will greatly benefit from setting boundaries and having an organized budget.

Home and Family Life

Sagittarius Moon may be a perpetual wanderer, exploring the world, refusing to settle down until they have examined all their options. Or they may want to focus on their studies and will only feel at home on a college campus or even in a monastery (their search for wisdom is strong!). Or Sagittarius Moon may simply not overthink it and make themselves at home wherever they are. Whatever the case may be, their home is an eclectic collection of the souvenirs they have gathered on their journeys. There is usually music and incense smoke in the air, with touches of their spiritual faith scattered throughout.

They often live in a large home and love having a large closet. Because they are so busy, they often wear whatever their hand grabs first, but it often ends up looking great anyway—it's that Sagittarius Moon luck. They love a deal when they go shopping, but they adore high fashion labels too.

They need space! And if their space is small, the windows and doors are likely to be open so they don't feel too hemmed in. They crave flow; they cannot get comfortable where there is stagnation. If they have a housemate or partner who is glued to the couch for days on end, they might get irritable, as they are happiest living with creative types with busy social lives.

Growing up, their greatest wish was to find a secret door in their home that led to another world. The Moon symbolizes safety, and Sagittarius Moon finds comfort through expanding their mind and spirit. Their childhood bedroom had shelves filled with books and movies about faraway lands and fantasy worlds, and their walls were decorated with posters of places and celebrities whose aesthetic mirrored their love of the whimsical, mystical, and unexpected. They enjoyed camping and sleeping under the stars, and dreamed about traveling far and wide.

There may have been an "anything goes" or "whatever works" approach to home life while they were growing up; however, there also may have been a blurring of boundaries. Their caregivers may have been charitable and giving, but also could have been swept up in a movement, dogma, or belief system, which the Sagittarius Moon child had to make sense of. They may have moved frequently or had many friends and family members whose houses they could also think of as their own. A "what's mine is yours" attitude in their early life fostered generosity, but they also needed to learn to set boundaries around giving more than they had. As a child, Sagittarius Moon was likely the sibling who wanted to eat chocolate ice cream when everyone else wanted strawberry. They had a contrarian edge, but were also the best at coming up with games during boring rainy days. They were usually the ones who knew how to fix broken toys, and when they were older, the Wi-Fi.

As a parent, Sagittarius Moon wants their children to be able to experience as much as possible, giving them lessons in whatever the child is interested in, and encouraging them to travel and enjoy their freedom. They are rather lenient, as they value independence, as long as their child does well in school or at least shows a passion for knowledge.

At Work

Sagittarius Moon has a deep desire to do something important for the world, to be of service. The Moon symbolizes safety, and they feel whole when in a career that benefits the greater good. They are fantastic communicators, so they may end up being a teacher or writer, or with a career in publishing. Knowledge is an important theme in Sagittarius Moon's life, and in their work, they will make sure they are spreading information far and wide, perhaps as an investigative journalist or a college educator.

Sagittarius Moon is adventurous and loves to travel, so they often incorporate that into their career. Even though they are spontaneous in many areas of life, when it comes to work, they are highly organized, love a routine, and do not leave town without an itinerary. Sagittarius Moon does not like to waste time when they are on the clock!

If you have a Sagittarius Moon boss, you might be surprised about how thorough and exacting they are when they seem so carefree in other areas of life. But you will have a brave and brilliant mentor at your disposal, always willing to give sage advice. If you have a Sagittarius Moon employee, they might occasionally have an aura of last night's party on them, but they will be one of the most impressive, intelligent people you could ever have on your team, and they will not let outside fun distract them from getting the job done.

Friendships

Sagittarius Moon is charming and easily amasses a large circle of friends. You would think that, with so many names in their address book, they would have a hard time keeping up with people; however, this Moon sign loves sending holiday letters and staying in touch with friends. Nothing makes them giddy like sticking a stamp on a vacation postcard and sending it off in a mailbox.

Sagittarius Moon has an easy, open energy, making them quite approachable. If you want to strike up a conversation and aren't sure what to say, just invite them to play a game of pool or join in a toast. They love a friendly, competitive spirit and a good celebration. Sagittarius Moon sometimes harbors a deep fear that they are not living life to the fullest, so invite them to do something exuberant with you.

There are two sides to this mutable Fire sign. While Sagittarius is a zodiac sign famous for being a blunt communicator, the truth is that they deeply value good manners and expect a level of decorum in their social circle. They will send thank-you cards and expect you to answer invitations promptly. Because fair give-and-take in relationships is so important to them, don't just call them when you want to vent or gossip; be sure to inquire about how they are doing. Sagittarius Moon is a deep thinker and values friendships that are built on a mutual passion for knowledge and intellectual and spiritual growth.

Love and Compatibility

Fortune favors the bold, and Sagittarius Moon is not one to stand shyly at a party: If they like you, they will walk right up and start a conversation. Sagittarius Moon can talk to just about anyone! They are usually attracted to well-read social butterflies who know where the coolest parties are and with whom they can have late-night debates about everything from pop culture to the meaning of life. They are smart, sexy, easygoing, and engaged in their community, with a curious spirit. They enjoy someone who plays a little hard to get and has a cheerful yet mysterious air about them. Sagittarius Moon enjoys the process of getting to know someone—if a partner can maintain the light, flirtatious banter that is so common in the beginning of any relationship and carry it on throughout the partnership, Sagittarius Moon will be in heaven.

What makes Sagittarius Moon feel safe in a relationship is open and honest communication. Their biggest fear in a partnership is being lied to or treated unfairly. They feel strongly about justice and will not tolerate being in a relationship where undue blame comes their way. When it comes to lies, they accept that anyone (themself included!) may tell white lies here and there—we are only human. But the idea that a partner is leading a double life or living a lie in some way is a true horror story for this moralizing Moon sign. While it might seem like Sagittarius Moon is resistant to commitment, the truth is that they just like to get to know someone well first, as a friend, so they can avoid players and tricksters.

Sagittarius Moon's dream date is one where they are unexpectedly swept off their feet. They can imagine nothing better than randomly running into a crush, spontaneously deciding to check out a neighborhood art gallery, then getting some dinner at a new restaurant they have been eager to try. Then, of course, an evening of passion ensues . . . and no one expected it to happen! This sort of adventure is exactly what makes Sagittarius Moon's heart sing, so if you are planning a date, keep your plans flexible, as the best times with them will happen on a whim.

Having fun is one of Sagittarius Moon's core emotional needs, and there is no one they have a blast with like **Aries Moon**. These two know how to celebrate life, and nearly every day is a party for them. Their intellectual connection is especially strong; Aries Moon adores what a philosopher Sagittarius Moon is. There is a physical, fiery passion between them that makes for a thrilling time in the bedroom.

Taurus Moon and Sagittarius Moon could spend all day shopping and dining. Both of these signs have a decadent edge to them; however, Sagittarius Moon can learn a lot from Taurus Moon about spending wisely. Taurus Moon enjoys many great adventures with this Fire sign and may even overcome some fears. Their love life is highly physical, and Taurus Moon's slow, seductive approach is sure to get Sagittarius Moon going.

Gemini is opposite Sagittarius on the zodiac wheel, so these two Moon signs are absolutely magnetized by each other. **Gemini Moon** is similar to Sagittarius Moon in that communication is so important to them. However, Sagittarius Moon may make overgeneralizations about Gemini Moon's feelings or intentions, and Gemini Moon can be critical. Being considerate is the key to a successful relationship, and their communication skills make this pair winners in the bedroom.

Free-spirited Sagittarius Moon does not always have a solid routine, but when they do, they feel much more nourished and grounded. In a relationship with **Cancer Moon**, they will learn how to cultivate daily practices. This partnership will find both Moon signs breaking bad habits. Cancer Moon adores Sagittarius Moon's openheartedness, and Sagittarius Moon delights in Cancer Moon's sense of humor. Caring Cancer Moon is much rowdier in bed than Sagittarius Moon expects, which is a delightful surprise!

Because these Fire signs are such showoffs, it is obvious to everyone when **Leo Moon** and Sagittarius Moon are flirting. They both understand the other's desire to be seen and appreciated. Leo Moon loves to lounge in bed, like a lion; however, they have a few moves that others might be too shy to attempt, which is sure to wow Sagittarius Moon. And, if Leo Moon is looking for drama in the bedroom, Sagittarius Moon knows exactly how to bring it.

Virgo Moon and Sagittarius Moon have very different approaches to their emotional life, but differences attract. Virgo Moon's careful nature inspires dashing Sagittarius Moon to have a gentler approach to life, and Sagittarius Moon's aura of grandness reminds Virgo Moon that there are many opportunities waiting to be explored. In the bedroom, Virgo Moon has a naughty side that totally takes Sagittarius Moon by surprise (and this Moon sign does love surprises!).

Sagittarius Moon adores **Libra Moon**—they are so stylish and popular, it is hard not to notice them. They share a fulfilling social life and a deep desire to be out in the world, meeting people and cultivating ideas. Their strong intellectual connection and solid friendship is the foundation of their relationship. They both deeply value justice and doing the correct thing. In the bedroom, they enjoy experimenting and likely have an exciting toy collection.

Who is more mysterious than **Scorpio Moon**? Always the seeker, Sagittarius Moon can't resist them and wants to learn all their secrets. At the same time, Sagittarius Moon will have to explore their own mysterious depths, and they'll learn so much through this union. Scorpio Moon adores Sagittarius Moon's straightforwardness about what they like in bed, while Sagittarius Moon swoons for Scorpio Moon's imagination, especially when it comes to sharing fantasies.

Their faith in love carries two **Sagittarius Moons** to their happily ever after. They believe anything is possible, and with such open hearts, it is hard for them not to end up where they want to be. There is plenty of trust, freedom, and adventure in this relationship. This is a cheerful partnership, with open communication and plenty of spontaneous shows of affection. They both have a dramatic approach to lovemaking, and it is likely to be quite loud, so they should live far away from neighbors if they can.

Can serious **Capricorn Moon** and jokester Sagittarius Moon fall in love? Indeed, they can! Capricorn Moon creates a sense of security that grounds Sagittarius Moon. Capricorn Moon is cautious, but they enjoy spoiling those they love. Sagittarius Moon is deeply generous, and these two are quite giving with each other. Their sex life is very intense: Sagittarius Moon encourages Capricorn Moon to open up and explore new desires.

Aquarius Moon and Sagittarius Moon form a fast friendship that is the foundation for a fantastic relationship. Rebellious Aquarius Moon has huge respect for Sagittarius Moon's guts. They both value freedom in their relationships, and neither has patience for inauthentic people. They are both honest about who they are, and because they have easy communication, they can navigate relationship issues quite smoothly. Their good communication also keeps their sex life interesting for a long time!

Sagittarius Moon feels at home with **Pisces Moon**. Sagittarius Moon is not always the nostalgic type, but they become a dreamy lover with Pisces Moon; suddenly, they start saving each movie ticket stub and scrapbooking each love note. Pisces Moon admires Sagittarius Moon's go-getter attitude, and it makes them feel safe to be with someone so brave and confident. Between the sheets, Pisces Moon's nurturing approach combines with Sagittarius Moon's spontaneity, making for a passionate and caring combination.

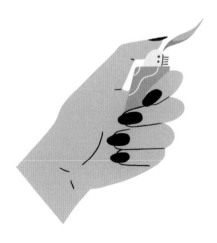

Progressed Moon

After a period of profound emotional rebirth as the Moon progressed through Water sign Scorpio, the Moon enters Fire sign Sagittarius, marking a period of emotional expansion. This is an exciting time in our education, perhaps coinciding with a graduation or a return to school. We may step into teaching roles at this time, and as we share our knowledge, we gain an even deeper understanding of life through the insights of our students. The progressed Moon in Sagittarius finds us eagerly spreading messages that are meaningful to us and may find us publishing some exciting work.

This is a period of exploration on every level, as we seek to grow in spiritual and intellectual knowledge, in our intimate relationships, and in our experiences of the world, whether that's through travel or simply trying something new off the menu at one of our favorite restaurants. Life has so much to offer, so why limit ourselves? We will examine our tendencies to overindulge, generalize, and take risks—and learn lessons about optimism and faith.

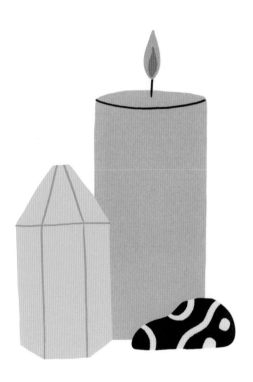

CAPRICORN MOON

Capricorn is a cardinal Earth sign ruled by the planet Saturn

Traditional astrologers regard the Moon in Capricorn as being in its "detriment," meaning stoic Capricorn is not an ideal placement for the Moon to cozy up in—but this doesn't surprise Capricorn Moon at all, because they're quite pessimistic: "Of course the Moon doesn't like being in the sign I have, that's life!" They are also sarcastic, hardworking (like a goat climbing up a mountain, Capricorn Moon is focused on reaching the top), and a touch devilish. Even if they see the glass as half empty, Capricorn Moon has filled that glass with quite a rare, decadent, hard-won elixir.

Like an old gothic estate, Capricorn Moon has plenty of antiques, a few intriguing family secrets, and a magnetic, stately aura. They have detailed accounts of names, birthdates, and deaths listed in the covers of a religious text or family album; Capricorn Moon knows the past well but is not sentimental about it. They know nothing lasts forever. But are they icing out their emotions? Or are they jaded? Great at compartmentalizing? Perhaps they are enlightened? Any of these options may be the answer, depending on where Capricorn Moon is in life and how deeply they have explored their inner world.

Capricorn is a materially minded Earth sign that wants to make good use of things—and what good use can you make of changeable, messy, vulnerable emotions? When Capricorn Moon learns that connection with their feelings leads to greater embodiment and healing, they will no longer see emotions as useless obstacles but as ladders that lead to higher understanding. The tarot card associated with Capricorn is the Devil, a reminder to consider long-term consequences and keep worldly things in the right perspective. It's important that Capricorn Moon learns that money isn't everything and they can't take it with them once this life is over.

Going Deeper

Wise Capricorn Moon has a deep respect for their own feelings and the feelings of others, but the immature Capricorn Moon may regard emotions in general as petty, pointless, or even a personal flaw. Capricorn Moon may ask themself, "Can't people just power through their day without being bogged down by fears and desires?" Stuffing feelings away in an attempt to be tough or because it is "childish" to cry is not going to lead to long-term happiness, even if it seems like the easier choice in the moment. It is OK to have feelings! Capricorn Moon can learn how to ride their emotions by journaling, speaking to counselors and loved ones, and connecting with their body (massage and other ways to relax are crucial for this Earth sign). It is simply more effective to feel emotions than ignore them!

Capricorn is associated with austerity due to being ruled by taskmaster Saturn, the planet of responsibilities, fears, and limitations, which is why it is so important for Capricorn Moon to be gentle with themself and others. Capricorn Moon also has lessons to learn about boundaries: Are they building walls so they do not have to deal with difficult emotions, or are they truly setting healthy, helpful parameters? They may need to figure out how to repair relationships after a spat with a friend or lover. If they can make friends with people who model how to bounce back after a disappointment, even better. Capricorn Moon finds healing in friends who demonstrate a fluid approach to life.

Home and Family Life

Capricorn Moon can fall into the habit of breakfast on the go and dinner at the computer, forgetting how much they enjoy slowing down and being at the table with their loved ones. However, when they do dive into home life, their space's decorations may have some childlike whimsy, whether it is splashes of color or plenty of games and trinkets. Astrologers say that Capricorns age in reverse, and this is true for Capricorn Moon too: They bring a youthful quality into the home.

As a partner or a housemate, organized Capricorn Moon will maintain a detailed chore chart that is faithfully updated. They tend to look after domestic chores quickly and efficiently; Capricorn is ruled by disciplined Saturn, after all! Capricorn Moon is famous for their patience, but they may get snippy when a home renovation moves too slowly or a lover takes too long to get ready for brunch. They enjoy living in cities, where they can have quick access to what they need, but also enjoy the space, privacy, and nature the country provides.

Capricorn Moon typically grew up with hardworking caregivers who may have worked from home or were often at their workplace, perhaps bringing the Capricorn Moon child along. The Capricorn Moon child's experience of seeing caregivers focused on business and presenting themselves professionally left a lasting impression. With caregivers frequently working or otherwise occupied with public life, the Capricorn Moon child may have felt unsure about when or how to share their emotions or ask for what they needed. They certainly had to mature quickly—being "grown up" is a strong Capricorn theme.

As a parent, Capricorn Moon seeks to inspire their children to have a strong work ethic, and they delight in teaching them how to negotiate.

Their childhood rooms were likely filled with trophies and posters of people they admired, their decor a reflection of the adult they saw themself as. They found inspiration in books and movies about great battles, warriors, or high achievers. Because Capricorn Moon knew adversity from a young age, people who have overcome and *won* inspire them. If you have a Capricorn Moon sibling, you likely spent plenty of time discussing deep and important things, and the meaning of life was a regular topic. As a young teenager, they may have been exceptionally angsty and worn lots of black. Or, eager to grow up and be taken seriously by adults, they may have dressed as if they were heading to the office—the Capricorn Moon child is ready to leave the house and do their own thing as quickly as possible. By the end of their teens, Capricorn Moon's fashion taste may have swung more DIY or retro than goth, but one thing's certain for Capricorn Moon at any age: They feel very at home in luxury garments!

At Work

Capricorn Moon enjoys working—perhaps too much so! They would do well to create a healthy separation between the office and their home. If they work from home (which they often enjoy), they will need to make sure their office feels very separate from the rest of their living space. If they go to a workplace, they likely feel very gratified by the physical space they carve out for themself, whether it is an ultra-organized craft station or a corner office with big windows (every Capricorn Moon's dream).

Because Capricorn Moon loves to work with and on behalf of people, they make great lawyers, advocates, and counselors. They are also trendsetters, and do well in fashion and beauty; they understand the "time" they are living in, and get what people of the moment want. The Capricorn archetype is known as being the "boss" of the zodiac—and being ruled by responsible Saturn, it makes sense. Part of the reason why Capricorn Moon makes a great boss is because they are excellent at giving constructive feedback, sandwiching a criticism between sincere compliments, and giving helpful pointers on how to do better.

As an employee, Capricorn Moon is a great team player and often known for their diplomacy in solving interpersonal issues at the office. While they can be quite grumpy in everyday life, Capricorn Moon knows how to put on a smile when they are at work . . . and it's genuine! They sincerely love what they do, which is an excellent asset to have in an employee. The Moon symbolizes what makes us feel safe, and for Capricorn Moon, it's knowing that they are building a legacy and having an effect on the world.

Friendships

Capricorn Moon may be one of the wildest friends you will ever have. They put such pressure on themselves to *be good* that when they can finally breathe easy and let loose, they swing very far in the other direction, being especially naughty!

Because Capricorn Moon may have had a strict upbringing, or may have put a lot of pressure on themself to be responsible when they were young, as they get older, they may be up for all-night ragers long after their friends have outgrown them. This often means an older Capricorn Moon has a bunch of younger friends to go clubbing with, just like a younger Capricorn Moon may have plenty of older friends with whom to play chess at reasonable hours.

They are often attracted to friends who are rebellious or mysterious in some way or who are VIPs but don't flaunt their clout in an obvious fashion. If you are enigmatic and successful, Capricorn Moon will want to connect with you. Capricorn Moon has a hard time trusting show-offs, even if they find them entertaining, but they do value friends who work as hard as they do.

Capricorn Moon seeks out relationships with people who are quite emotionally intense. These deep-feeling friends help Capricorn Moon recognize (and respect!) their own powerful feelings. In turn, Capricorn Moon helps their friends stay grounded in reality, rather than getting lost in fantasies and paranoia. You'll seek out your Capricorn Moon friend when you don't want things sugarcoated, when you need honesty and the attention of someone who won't theorize about bright sides. They will stand with you in the truth of your situation, acknowledging the weight of your emotions and shouldering it with you as they validate your experience.

Love and Compatibility

Capricorn Moon is a serious sign, and they approach everything with careful consideration, especially romance. They find it difficult to open up until their partner has shown that they can hold safe space for them. Emotional abandonment is one of their greatest fears, as they have experienced it before and are guarded against it happening again.

Capricorn Moon is a lusty, sensual, devoted, responsible partner who admires deeply emotional people. They are attracted to nurturing types, and it is a bonus if their companion knows their way around a kitchen. Tradition is important to Capricorn Moon, but can also be a touchy subject. They seek to break free from much of their past or their family's history and may need to heal inherited trauma or end unhealthy cycles of behavior. Because of this, they value a partner with whom they can explore both new and lost or forgotten traditions.

Capricorn Moon typically has a dry sense of humor, and as hilarious as they can be, they sometimes have a hard time loosening up. Because of this, they are often very attracted to gregarious, easygoing people who can joke about anything with anyone. They find healing in people who are in touch with their intuition and can share their feelings freely. While it can take a while for Capricorn Moon to open up, being with a trusting (and trustworthy!) sensitive partner makes all the difference. They need someone who can balance their sometimes stern form of expression with flexibility and forgiveness.

Can't get Capricorn Moon out of a grumpy mood? Be in one yourself. Misery loves company, and nothing will cheer up Capricorn Moon like knowing they have someone they can complain with. In their overly responsible minds, they often feel like they are the only ones worried about the state of the world, and they need to know that you care too.

Commitment is not a problem for Capricorn Moon, as they do nearly everything for keeps, but they are very hesitant to rely on someone other than themself and are cautious about who they invest in emotionally. They tend not to rush into partnerships and value taking things slowly. The Moon symbolizes what makes us feel comfortable, and for the Capricorn archetype whose sign is ruled by Saturn, the planet of time, that is exactly what is needed: time with a person.

With **Aries Moon**, Capricorn Moon finds someone who reminds them of home. Even though they may seem different (with Capricorn Moon approaching things cautiously while Aries Moon jumps into action), there is a familiarity, even nostalgia, that arises when they connect. Aries Moon's competitive nature is exciting to Capricorn Moon, and there is a lot of sexual chemistry between these two. Though they might feel like they have something to prove to each other, these issues can be worked out in the bedroom!

When Capricorn Moon falls in love with **Taurus Moon** (which is quite easy for them to do, as they are both sensual Moon signs), they are in it for the long haul. Both of these Moon signs are cautious about rushing into things, and they are relieved when they meet someone as thoughtful about commitment as they are. These two can luxuriate in bed all day—Capricorn Moon rarely is inspired to lounge naked all day, but with Taurus Moon, it just happens!

Hardworking Capricorn Moon and playful **Gemini Moon** can be great influences on each other, but Gemini Moon craves verbal affirmations while Capricorn Moon needs to be shown love through actions. They are both problem solvers, and through solid communication, they can give each other what they need, especially in the bedroom! They may need to make some adjustments at first, but Capricorn Moon loves to give directions and Gemini Moon loves to accommodate them.

Intuitive Cancer is the opposite sign of industrious Capricorn, but when Capricorn Moon connects with **Cancer Moon**, it is a love for the ages, thanks to their deep spiritual connection. Cancer Moon may be stuck in the past, and Capricorn Moon worried about the future, but together they may be able to find peace in the present—that is, if they can compromise on their many differences. Opposites attract, especially in the bedroom for these two.

Leo Moon is flashy in a way that may make Capricorn Moon feel bashful. These two Moon signs have different needs, but they can encourage each other to step out of their comfort zones, and this is often an emotionally transformative relationship for Capricorn Moon. They both enjoy the finer things in life, which is where they find common ground. Warm and generous Leo Moon has an uncanny ability to coax out Capricorn Moon's secret desires, which makes for an exciting sex life.

With **Virgo Moon**, Capricorn Moon feels a relief—finally, someone as discerning as they are! Capricorn Moon adores Virgo Moon's analytical mind, but these two also have lots of fun together and have the same sense of humor. Capricorn Moon's brand of lusty sex appeal is exactly what Virgo Moon craves. Their sex life is absolutely wild; do not think for a second that these two seemingly buttoned-up signs can't loosen up together; their chemistry is off the charts.

Capricorn Moon is attracted to **Libra Moon**'s grace and popularity. They have different emotional needs, but they both enjoy negotiating, so they can work things out as long as Libra Moon can be decisive and Capricorn Moon can resist being sarcastic. There is a magnetic attraction between them sexually. Capricorn Moon enjoys impressing Libra Moon in bed, and Libra Moon loves to be impressed!

Capricorn Moon thinks creative **Scorpio Moon** is just the coolest. These Moon signs have hard edges but are able to share their softness easily with each other, making for an emotionally fulfilling relationship. They each respect the other's maturity and cautious approach to things. Their sex life is always exciting, as these two enjoy trying new things together. Scorpio Moon loves thrills, and Capricorn Moon loves that about them.

When Capricorn Moon meets **Sagittarius Moon**, everything they thought they knew about love goes out the window. Sagittarius Moon is very blunt, but even so, Capricorn Moon finds them so mysterious. Sagittarius Moon loves being spoiled by Capricorn Moon and appreciates how hardworking Capricorn Moon is, making the gifts they receive so much more meaningful. Love is a whole new adventure and learning experience, and they may learn things in bed they never may have considered trying!

With fellow **Capricorn Moon**, there is an instant connection, a "boss recognizes boss" sort of vibe. It is a pleasure for them to share the fruits of their labor with someone as industrious as they are. They may be tempted to start a business together, and as successful as it may be, it is imperative that they spend time together outside the office too. They both have a mischievous side and enjoy being naughty in the bedroom.

With **Aquarius Moon**, Capricorn Moon meets someone who shares their focus and drive, and values many of the same things regarding security and comfort, but who lives life with a bold, fearless approach. They love setting and accomplishing goals for the future as a team. They can both be quite aloof, but the passage of time will prove their attraction, and many wild nights can take place between them.

Capricorn Moon would seemingly grow tired of **Pisces Moon**'s absurd sense of humor and easygoing ways—false, they absolutely adore it! They have a strong friendship and intellectual connection. Capricorn Moon can overwork themselves, but Pisces Moon helps them take breaks. It's a healing experience for Capricorn Moon to be with someone who gives so freely and doesn't "keep score." Pisces Moon can keep up with all of Capricorn Moon's exciting sexual fantasies.

Progressed Moon

The exuberance and growth experience during the progressed Moon's time in Sagittarius moves into a period of discernment, consolidating, and building as the Moon progresses into Capricorn. We accumulated and disseminated knowledge during the progressed Moon's time in Sagittarius, but it is no longer time for talk when the progressed Moon is in materially focused Earth sign Capricorn. It is time for action. An anything-goes, follow-our-passion vibe transforms into a structured, focused one. We begin to look at the past realistically, giving up on romanticizing what was, and we are driven to build a better future for ourselves, with more security and success. We might find ourselves reflecting on what we want our legacies to be, as we are looking for meaning and contemplating existential questions concerning time and purpose.

Responsibility is a major theme during this period. We may get promotions where we are managing others, overseeing projects, or being the person others look to for direction. In our emotional lives, we may be less willing to let in new people who have not proven that they live up to our standards and support our goals. While the progressed Moon is in Capricorn, we may feel like it's "lonely at the top," so we do what we can to lift others up!

AQUARIUS
MOON

Aquarius is a fixed Air sign ruled by the planets Saturn and Uranus

Whoever said Aquarius Moon is unfeeling or uninterested in their emotional life has misunderstood a core aspect of the Aquarian experience: the fascination with mystery. And what is more mysterious than emotions? Aquarius Moon doesn't just have feelings; they have thoughts, questions, and *feelings* about their feelings! Aquarius has a scientific mind, and Aquarius Moon might have a detached air about them, but do not be fooled into thinking it is because they are unaffected—they are deeply curious.

Aquarius is ruled by Saturn, the planet of boundaries and reality, and Uranus, the planet of surprise and innovation. Together, these two planets speak to this Moon sign's creative ability to take old structures and transform them into something new. The Moon symbolizes safety and security, so Aquarius Moon feels most comfortable when they are changing paradigms. Aquarius Moon has big visions for the future, and this is reflected in the Star, the tarot card that is associated with Aquarius. The Star symbolizes hope, and Aquarius Moon knows that things that seem impossible can be overcome.

It is incredibly meta to have the Moon (a symbolic container of emotions) in an Air sign whose symbol is the water bearer (Water being the element that rules emotion and "bearer" meaning "one who carries"). So, is this Moon sign ultra-emotional? Not any more or less than anyone else. Even though Aquarius has the reputation of being cool and detached, this Moon sign's emotions run deep. Aquarius Moon may be one of the most introspective people you know. As an Air sign, they have an intellectual approach to emotional life: If they have a feeling that does not make sense to them, they will hash it out in their journal or over the phone with a friend. They are a fixed sign too, which gives them a focused, even stubborn quality. They know what they want, as they have spent *a lot* of time thinking about it.

Going Deeper

Subversive Moon sign Aquarius cannot cozy up to conformity. Aquarius is often thought of as the rebel of the zodiac, and this Moon sign delights in being edgy and different. They are a freethinker but may have struggled to gain their independence after growing up in a family or location where fitting in was expected. For them, freedom to express their individuality is key. Aquarius Moon thinks a lot about power and how to redistribute it. They have a keen understanding and dislike of how people can become greedy for control and dominance. This Moon sign will not be bossed around. When they were young, they were so rebellious that they might have fooled themself into thinking they were above heartbreak or sadness. But as they mature, they realize that denying emotions does not get rid of them, it simply represses them.

While their social life and the scene they belong to is like a second home to Aquarius Moon, they are also very introspective and often need time to sit with their feelings. However, sometimes they may retreat for too long and end up in a rut, so it is important for them to establish varied routines. Aquarius Moon would be wise to make time for some fresh air and movement. Being a fixed Air sign, they can get so focused on the task at hand that scheduling breaks can be helpful. They might think sitting in a bathtub with scented candles is the cure to their problems (and sometimes it is), but if this method is not working for them lately, they might try running to the coffee shop to say hi to friends, picking up a new book at their favorite bookstore, or viewing the sunset with a loved one.

Home and Family Life

Step into Aquarius Moon's home and you will find state-of-the-art appliances that border on futuristic. They love things that are high-tech and luxurious! People might expect cool Aquarius to live in a sparse, cold environment; however, they have eclectic taste, they love to have "stuff," and coziness is extremely important to them. Touches of nature are everywhere: Cactus collections multiply on their windowsill, near their assortment of antique finds. Their space is filled with curiosities. While they love living in cities and enjoy the novelties and wide range of activities they offer, Aquarius Moon often craves connection with the earth, so living in a more rural area, where they can grow their own food or enjoy looking at an expanse of stars in the night sky, is fantastic for them. As important to them as their roomy, comfortable furniture is their at-home loungewear: They have a snuggly outfit for every day of the week, and their pajama collection is enviable.

Aquarius Moon is fun to have as a partner or housemate; they might spontaneously cook dinner or bring home something exciting and unexpected, like a popcorn machine or a massage chair. If you grew up with an Aquarius Moon sibling, you enjoyed fun, random moments where they returned home with spy gear, magic tricks, and other unlikely things. Still, you may have been on the receiving end of their short temper—Aquarius Moon is not too chill to get worked up now and then! Fortunately, this airy Moon sign values communication skills, and as they mature, they are less likely to snap and more able to hash things out.

When they were children, Aquarius Moon collected all sorts of trinkets and gadgets, many that glowed in the dark. They may have built their own computer, if their parents did not give them one; they are very resourceful and love electronics. Their parents may have been concerned about spoiling them, or perhaps there were no boundaries at all around what they could or could not have. Therefore, Aquarius Moon is conscious about having a healthy and balanced approach to generosity with themselves.

Their parents may have also gone through some noteworthy transformations while Aquarius Moon was growing up, which taught them that amazing changes can happen if one keeps an open mind. If they lacked support growing up, their rebellious edge may become even edgier, and maintaining their cool, aloof reputation can make their demeanor even icier. As an adult, it is important to them to create a peaceful, comfortable home, where everyone feels heard and supported. As a parent, they don't want to be the type who says, "When I was your age . . ." They want to be able to understand what their children are going through in *today's* world, not yesterday's.

At Work

Aquarius Moon is a brilliant researcher, problem solver, and innovator. Working in tech, or in any field where they interact one-on-one with clients, may call to them. They know how to make their clients feel important and are fantastic at helping them achieve their goals. Aquarius Moon may have fantasized about being a detective or a spy, and indeed, they would be great at it. Whatever they choose to do, they will likely create fantastic innovations in their field.

Aquarius Moon is a helpful teammate, although they might seem like loners at first. If an Aquarius Moon is your boss, you will find they have high expectations but are also inspiring mentors. As an employee, they are organized and great at taking initiative, but because of their independent streak, they need autonomy and cannot stand being micromanaged. They may even start their own business. Legacy is important to Aquarius Moon because they feel a deep need to effect change in the world and build a better future, and they have a deep desire to contribute something that will benefit generations to come.

Friendships

Because Aquarius Moon may have a detached aura about them, it can be intimidating to approach them; however, they adore connecting with gregarious, confident, and fun people. They are entertained by show-offs! In many ways, they are discreet. However, they do like to stand out in a crowd—they just prefer to be the one who decides when that happens, so don't start filming them at karaoke without their permission.

Aquarius Moon makes an excellent friend, and they always have something exciting or unusual for you to enjoy when you spend time together. They are not the type to gossip, but they are blunt when they need to be and are a great listener. They value straightforward communication and do not feel comfortable in friendships where things are not plainly discussed. If you are in a friendship with an Aquarius Moon, do not expect them to simply intuit how you feel; rather, they will expect you to clearly state your needs.

Aquarius Moon is usually very involved with hobbies and is likely to meet many of their friends through a scene they are immersed in or a club they belong to. They are into community organizing and have causes they are passionate about, and they expect the same in their friends. What they look for in friendships—and really in all their relationships—is to team up with people who have courage and strength.

Love and Compatibility

Aquarius Moon is magnetic and has no problem attracting partners: Their cool, detached approach to flirting is catnip for most of the human population. Few things stir someone with a crush to a greater frenzy than being unsure about how an individual feels about them, so many of Aquarius Moon's admirers have had their hearts tested by how nonchalant this airy Moon sign can be!

But there are a few signs that Aquarius Moon is interested: They will make an effort to hang out and be your friend, as friendship is an important foundation for their love relationships. They will also show an interest in your work, turning up at your art show or reading up on your field. They desire a partner who is passionate about their life and career, so if they invest in investigating what you do, that is definitely a sign they are intrigued. They will also give compliments. Aquarius Moon does not dish these out too freely, so it is noteworthy if you get some praise.

Although Aquarius Moon can be quiet, they are often attracted to popular, talkative people who always have something interesting to say, whether it's a historical fact, a philosophical observation, or some gossip. Aquarius Moon can be shy about emotional expression, which may be why they are so entranced by people with a dramatic flair who can externalize what is going on for Aquarius Moon internally. While some people find show-offs unattractive, Aquarius Moon can watch them all day! Aquarius Moon's type is theatrical and glamorous, and likes to party. Aquarius Moon seeks someone who knows how to celebrate life and is curious about the world; people who are jaded and lack passion are a turnoff. Aquarius Moon is often invested in a scene or community, and finding a partner with whom they can be a "power couple" is a big plus.

Aquarius Moon adores how spontaneous and bold **Aries Moon** is, and Aries Moon loves spending time with someone who is simply cool. Communication between freethinking Aquarius Moon and fearless Aries Moon is so harmonious that it is easy for these two to become best friends, and they often share an exciting social circle. They also enjoy a fulfilling sex life, as asking for what they need comes so naturally.

Aquarius Moon can build a cozy home with **Taurus Moon**, but Aquarius Moon has a rebellious streak and Taurus Moon has a stubborn one, so finding middle ground is important. Taurus Moon's decadence invites cool Aquarius Moon to enjoy life's pleasures, and Aquarius Moon's brilliance brings loads of creative inspiration to Taurus Moon. They have lots of chemistry in the bedroom: Taurus Moon helps Aquarius Moon slow down and really enjoy their senses.

Gemini Moon is so much fun for Aquarius Moon to be around; they are on the same wavelength about how to celebrate life, have fun, and unwind after a long day. Gemini Moon's playful nature is one of Aquarius Moon's favorite things about them, and Gemini Moon adores Aquarius Moon's philosophical side. As Air Moons, they value communication, and they're likely to be in touch all day. These two will rarely get bored of each other—especially in bed!

Nurturing **Cancer Moon** makes the sort of comfort food Aquarius Moon drools over; however, sweet energy in the kitchen is not enough to make a relationship work. Cancer Moon will need to clearly communicate their needs and Aquarius Moon will need to be more emotionally sensitive if these two want to make magic happen for the long term. Aquarius Moon's adventurous approach to sex delights imaginative Cancer Moon!

Leo is Aquarius's opposite sign, and with some compromise, a relationship between **Leo Moon** and Aquarius Moon can be very successful. They have different emotional needs, yet can complete each other rather nicely. For example, Leo Moon loves to be the center of attention and Aquarius Moon loves to be entertained—what a win-win! They are very passionate in the bedroom and eager to show off for each other.

Virgo Moon and Aquarius Moon have a surprising amount in common, especially with their shared down-to-earth approach to emotional life. However, both will have to make some adjustments; neither can deal with the other's bad habits. With a solid friendship between them, they can cheer each other on as they make amazing transformations and celebrate their victories together. They have a great time in the bedroom. While they both can be quite particular about what they like, they are eager to please!

While some may regard **Libra Moon** as indecisive and dainty, Aquarius Moon finds them totally stimulating. They cheer when Libra Moon's competitive streak makes an appearance, and they love debating with them. They learn so much from Libra Moon, and communication flows easily. Their emotional needs are aligned, especially around their craving for intellectual stimulation. They have wonderful sexual chemistry, and they know just how to take care of each other, in bed and out.

It might take a while for Aquarius Moon and **Scorpio Moon** to go on a date, due to how "cool" they like to play things, but eventually one thing leads to another, and suddenly, they've ended up in bed, where the energy between them is absolutely electric! Scorpio Moon is often described as intense, and Aquarius Moon has their own dash of intensity too; their relationship can lead to fantastic transformations in their lives.

Aquarius Moon has an easy time connecting with **Sagittarius Moon**, as their communication styles align and they have similar emotional needs. They both value adventure in their lives. The Moon is all about safety and security, but these two Moon signs find comfort when they are exploring their limits. They crave novelty and love to experiment, something evident in their sex life, which is anything but boring.

Aquarius Moon loves a mystery, so it is no surprise that they are attracted to **Capricorn Moon**, as this earthy Moon sign is a total puzzle to them. Each takes a serious approach to their emotional life, but Capricorn Moon may be more invested in tradition than Aquarius Moon, who is usually thinking about the future. In bed, they explore hidden desires, making this a thrilling union. Aquarius Moon would do well to spoil their Capricorn Moon lover with gifts.

Two **Aquarius Moons** in love will have an exceptionally exciting relationship! They both share a core need to experiment, and they will support each other's dreams and goals. If they share a hobby, they are sure to be the coolest couple in the scene, and if they have different hobbies, that's all good—they have someone to cheer them on as they explore their interests. They have intense sexual chemistry: As cool and aloof as they can be, in the bedroom the energy is anything but.

Aquarius Moon will learn much about generosity and abundance with **Pisces Moon**. Pisces Moon has a huge imagination, which is very attractive to this intellectual Air sign. Aquarius Moon has a logical way of relating to emotional life that differs from sensitive Pisces Moon, who may struggle with trust issues, but with love and communication, they can overcome any bumps in the road. Their sex life is adventurous, sweet, and grounding for both of them.

Progressed Moon

After reaching great heights while progressing through Capricorn, the Moon enters Air sign Aquarius, where it takes in the view. So much has been achieved! The progressed Moon in Aquarius asks what will be done with everything that has been gained. How can it be shared with others? Where can innovation take place?

The progressed Moon in Aquarius finds us in an experimental mood. We may dive deeper around an interest or a hobby. We may develop an interest in technology and invest in social causes. We may crave more time alone to immerse ourselves in our hobbies. We may also distance ourselves from some circles as we reconsider where we fit in. During this time, we form a deeper understanding of our boundaries and are better able to communicate our emotional needs. We may feel much less flexible about adjusting who we are to please other people: Who cares if other people think we are unusual?

PISCES
MOON

Pisces is a mutable Water sign ruled by the planets Jupiter and Neptune

The Moon in mystical Pisces makes for a powerful placement: deeply emotional, hugely creative, and totally otherworldly. There is a grandness to Pisces Moon, but there is also a vulnerability and flexibility. Pisces Moon is symbolized by the fish, and there is much going on beneath their waters. They are not only an intuitive Water sign but also an adaptable mutable sign. Pisces Moon is resilient: They have been through a lot in life and not always had the support they needed, but they typically trust that something greater is in store for them, and that keeps them going.

Pisces Moon feels most at home when they are touching other realms, whether that's reading a fantasy novel or spending time in deep meditation. Pisces Moon has a reputation for being sensitive and very emotional. They are also quite adventurous: They love to travel and learn, as they see these as opportunities for transformation. The tarot card associated with Pisces is the Moon, which is all about mystery and the unknown, a space Pisces Moon knows well. Pisces Moon is an expert at navigating the world using their intuition, but they must also find ways to stay grounded and not get swept up by imaginary dangers. They also need to keep firm boundaries, as they may take on other people's issues as their own.

The Moon is all about safety and security, but in Water sign Pisces, there is an understanding that things in life are not set in stone— water eventually erodes rock. While some people might find comfort in brick houses, Pisces Moon prefers to build a metaphorical home out of lighter material, one that moves with the wind and can be easily relocated or replaced. To some, this might seem like Pisces Moon is avoiding setting down roots, but this is not so; they simply feel most at home where movement can occur.

Going Deeper

Pisces Moon cares deeply about tending to others, but it is important they don't forget to pamper themself. Pisces is known to "check out"—it is a highly psychic sign that can easily become overwhelmed by vibes, which may mean they drift off to protect themself. This floaty Moon sign benefits from practices that help them sink into their body, such as massage, dance, a daily walk, or making love. Pedicures are a great place to start, since Pisces rules the feet and a basin of bubbly warm water relaxes just about anyone. Fantasy and magic are themes close to Pisces Moon's heart, so immersive theater and science-fiction films are wonderful ways for them to indulge their love of whimsy while staying grounded in reality.

Pisces Moon finds healing in making and enjoying art. Talking about their feelings is great, but working them out on a canvas, through poetry, or with their favorite musical instrument is important for their self-expression too. Pisces Moon also needs to have fun, as they can fall into slumps of weepiness from taking on the pain of others; they truly feel the weight of the world in their heart. They may be overcome by guilt for feeling happy when there is so much suffering in the world, so they need to make time to laugh and create joy. Once they tap into the healing power of creativity, realizing that happiness is not a selfish act, they can create amazing changes within themself and their whole community too, as they are excellent at spreading love and joy.

Expressing emotions is crucial for any Moon sign, but for this Water sign in particular, reflecting on their own history of being allowed to cry or being comforted when crying may be an important step toward healing. Pisces is ruled by two planets: expansive Jupiter and limitless Neptune. As mystical as these planets are, they are not too hot on boundaries! Jupiter seeks to expand limits, and Neptune blurs them. Learning about boundaries and structure in therapy can be completely transformative for this Moon sign.

Home and Family Life

Pisces Moon's childhood bedroom was likely filled with toys from fantasy films, and as an adult, this inclination toward whimsy persists. There's usually some incense wafting in the air and an eclectic vibe to the decor. Pisces Moon's home has enough books to rival Gemini's. There is no room for a mug on their coffee table, as it is too cluttered with books. Yes, clutter—there is lots of it in Pisces Moon's home, as they assign sentimental meaning to nearly every object they come across. The one area that is typically clear and organized is their home office.

Their kitchen is filled with gadgets they've experimented with a few times; however, for them, the kitchen is better served as a hot spot for tea and conversation with a friend. They usually have a few dishes they love to make, and if you are their partner or housemate, you will likely benefit from the treats they bring home after a day exploring a new neighborhood. They can get into a habit of frequent takeout when their lives get too busy, so making them a home-cooked meal is a fantastic way to show love and support.

Pisces Moon may have an easier time nurturing others than they do themself. When they overcome this tendency, they become a master of self-advocacy. Growing up, their parents may have assumed that Pisces Moon would learn to care for themself by osmosis, but just because this Moon sign is so intuitive does not mean they don't need guidance! Caretakers, teachers, and elders willing to answer Pisces Moon's many questions may have helped instill a sense of confidence in them.

As a child, Pisces Moon heard stories about family members who were well traveled and in the know. This legacy of knowing the best spots far and wide continued with Pisces Moon; even in their childhood days, they knew all the neighborhood hot spots for ice cream and lemonade. Much like how they know all the best galleries and restaurants now (which means they are often attracted to culturally rich cities, though they love the peace and calm of the countryside too). As a sibling, Pisces Moon found sharing their toys easier than not sharing opinions. They were happy to split dessert with you as long as you agreed with them. Their love of fantasy was evident in their clothing choices as a child, as their style had a whimsical flare. As an adult, they may use fashion as an art form.

As a parent, Pisces Moon often strives to be a teacher to their children, helping them understand how to care for themselves. Learning to deal with grief and endings early in life also deeply informs how they approach the world emotionally. For an adult Pisces Moon, home is not only where the heart is, but also where one goes to escape the troubles of the world, where magical realms can be enjoyed via books, movies, daydreams, and sleep.

At Work

Pisces Moon makes a brilliant teacher or guide. No matter what field they end up in, they have a broad-minded and generous approach to sharing their wisdom with colleagues, clients, and the public. Pisces Moon does not see the point in participating in something if it is not helpful, and they will not entertain a gig that does not contribute to the greater good. Pisces Moon sometimes has a reputation for being shy or mopey (being the last sign of the zodiac, Pisces is deep in their feelings, with quite a heavy energy); however, they are a fantastic motivational speaker and enjoy inspiring people. They often get involved in organizations that promote high ethical standards in their field.

Some may scrutinize go-with-the-flow Pisces Moon for being too easygoing; however, they are surprisingly organized at work. If they start their own business, Pisces Moon will pump themself up by making their workspace as glamorous as possible. They are not flashy, generally, but creating an atmosphere of opulence inspires their productivity. Self-employed or otherwise, the sometimes scattered Pisces Moon finds joy in everyday routines and the success their hard work brings them.

As a boss, Pisces Moon seeks to hire people who take initiative, as they do not like to micromanage. The workplace is one arena where their competitive side really shines. As an employee, humble Pisces Moon might surprise you by displaying their employee-of-the-month certificate on their desk.

Friendships

Do not be surprised that your daydreamer friend Pisces Moon is such a fantastic and present listener. Pisces Moon can have a reputation of being flighty when it comes to communication, but they can be a surprisingly grounded, receptive listener, putting their intuitive skills to good use. They are not fans of gossip, although they usually know what's going on with everyone, partly because of their sixth sense and partly because they are very well connected. This Moon sign attracts friends who are quite similar to them: people who have causes they are passionate about and with whom they can discuss their hopes and fears. Pisces Moon might get caught up in fantasy and paranoia, so they also need grounded folks who can nonjudgmentally reason with them and make them laugh.

Pisces Moon takes their social life seriously; it is basically a second career for them. In fact, their social life and career may blend quite a bit. Pisces Moon is friends with many VIPs and tends to gravitate toward friends with powerful careers. Pisces Moon wants their vision to come to life, and that is why they love teaming up with friends who know how to build things from the ground up.

If you are friends with a Pisces Moon, you will spend many evenings discussing art, spirituality, and social justice; you might even tie-dye something together or help them organize their crystal collection. Although this zodiac sign can be rather dreamy, that does not mean they laze away their days playing guitar in the park. They only do that on *some* days, while spending others connecting with friends whose industriousness and focus inspire and motivate them.

Love and Compatibility

Pisces Moon loves romance, yet is often drawn to practical types with a sharp, analytical mind. While Pisces Moon may doodle their crush's name in their notebook, their crush is doodling equations in theirs. Mystical, spiritual Pisces Moon falls in love with their whole heart for people who are just as caring as they are and just as invested and involved in their community. Pisces Moon looks for a down-to-earth and intelligent partner who can also entertain surreal ideas and wants to change the world for the better.

This Moon sign loves to stay up late listening to music or fantasizing about encounters with otherworldly beings, so their ideal partner is someone who is responsible and capable of waking up at 7 a.m. to walk the dog (in case Pisces Moon needs to sleep in). They dream of being with someone protective and nurturing who can care for them like Pisces Moon cares for so many others. Spiritual connection is also highly important to Pisces Moon; for them, this means being honest, vulnerable, and faithful in a relationship, and, especially, believing in one another.

Pisces Moon loves little escapes, so a great date might entail a picnic in a hidden garden or a getaway to the beach so they can spend time near their element, Water. A spa day is another great option, as is theater, especially if the show is musical, colorful, or fantastical in some way. But the most important thing to Pisces Moon is to feel like they can easily share their emotions with their partner, and that their partner will reciprocate. Pisces Moon will enjoy nearly any activity for date night so long as it involves deep conversation and emotional receptivity. Pisces Moon is deeply emotional and cannot be neglected in that regard.

Pisces Moon is enamored by **Aries Moon**'s courage and confidence. This sensitive Water Moon loves being protected and cherished by this Fire Moon. They are both very generous with each other. Aries Moon is a straightforward kind of person and is intrigued by dreamy Pisces Moon's air of mystery. A lover of the chase, Aries Moon has an approach that delights kittenish Pisces Moon, making for a passionate energy in the bedroom.

With **Taurus Moon**, friendship comes naturally. Many would describe Taurus as a stubborn Earth sign, but Pisces Moon just doesn't see it! Pisces Moon's creativity inspires Taurus Moon, and Taurus Moon's stability grounds Pisces Moon. Taurus Moon's luxurious approach to life feels right to this go-with-the-flow Moon sign. Pisces Moon really brings out the chill side of Taurus Moon. Plus, their sex life is always evolving thanks to their great communication skills.

Gemini Moon is in awe of Pisces Moon's intuition and imagination, and Pisces Moon admires how Gemini Moon can spot a flaw in any plan. These two feel at home with each other. They both crave flexibility and freedom in their lives, but have different emotional approaches (Gemini Moon may ask many questions while Pisces Moon hides for cover), which they can overcome through communication and patience. They have an intense sexual chemistry.

It is so easy for Pisces Moon to fall in love with **Cancer Moon**. Not only do their emotional needs align, but they also enjoy having fun and partying. They are best friends, celebrating the good times and supporting each other through the bad times. Their sex life is emotionally intense and fulfilling, especially because it's so easy for them to be honest with each other about what they desire.

Leo Moon's superstar influence inspires Pisces Moon to break bad habits and be their most polished self. Fortunately, Pisces Moon is flexible and enjoys change, unlike Leo Moon, who can be quite fixed in their ways! Leo Moon has a deep urge to be creative. They cannot rest unless they are producing art, and this pair can create incredible things together. Pisces Moon adores Leo Moon's theatrical, dramatic approach to sex, and Leo Moon loves being the subject of Pisces Moon's erotic poetry.

Virgo is Pisces's opposite sign, so when Pisces Moon falls in love with **Virgo Moon**, they will have very different ideas about what constitutes safety and comfort. Still, they have tremendous respect for each other and a desire to meet halfway. Both of these signs love to help people, so they help each other greatly. Plus, they have an exciting sex life, as Virgo Moon's sensuality meshes beautifully with Pisces Moon's whimsy.

With **Libra Moon**, Pisces Moon is challenged to take a different approach to their emotional life. Both of these Moon signs can be indecisive, but Libra Moon is concerned with making the right choice, while Pisces Moon is overwhelmed by all the choices. These two will stay up late having many philosophical debates, and will challenge each other to change and grow. Their sex life is imaginative and deeply intimate.

Pisces Moon is often immediately attracted to **Scorpio Moon**, someone who is as philosophical and emotionally intense as they are.

Scorpio is the sign of transformation, and with them, Pisces Moon breaks free from all sorts of limiting paradigms, while Scorpio Moon basks in Pisces Moon's fun, creative energy. Plus, their sexual chemistry is remarkable! These two Water Moon signs can't keep their hands off each other: They both find comfort in emotional connection and intimacy.

Pisces Moon finds plenty of fun and adventure with **Sagittarius Moon**, but they have to be careful not to overindulge in spending, sweets, or whatever their fancy is. They have differing emotional needs (Sagittarius Moon wants to run off for an adventure right now, while Pisces Moon wants to hang back for meditation practice), but are both open-minded enough to work things out. They have a decadent approach to pleasure, which benefits them in the bedroom.

Capricorn Moon has a grounded quality to them that makes Pisces Moon feel safe. Capricorn Moon is more materially minded than spiritual Pisces Moon, but their difference in this regard benefits them both: Pisces Moon has someone solid to lean on, and Capricorn Moon has a wonderfully intuitive and imaginative partner. They have an easy friendship and fulfilling sex life, as Capricorn Moon is up for whatever Pisces Moon wants to try. These two love to experiment together.

Whom does Pisces Moon find a total mystery? None other than **Aquarius Moon**. Pisces Moon is deeply introspective, and with Aquarius Moon, they will learn new things about themself. They both have a deep inner desire to explore the mysteries of the universe, leading to intriguing late-night conversations. Aquarius Moon is fantastic at drawing out Pisces Moon's most secret desires, making this an exciting pair in the bedroom. Pisces Moon's generous spirit makes Aquarius Moon feel soft and sentimental.

When together, two **Pisces Moons** find that they can be completely themselves: wonderfully silly, full of imagination, and brimming with deep emotion. There is an alignment around emotional needs: freedom and flexibility plus support and understanding. They both wish for true love and believe in the best in people, even when life has been hard. They are a creative couple and have wonderful sexual chemistry, eager to dive deep around pleasure and give generously to each other.

Progressed Moon

After the Moon leaves cool Air sign Aquarius, it plunges into Pisces's deep waters. The pendulum swings from detached to immersed as the progressed Moon enters this deeply emotional sign. This is a tremendous moment for exploring spirituality, emotions, intimacy, and new, profound ways of connecting with others, perhaps through more conscious lovemaking or group therapy. We may feel more wistful and sentimental than usual. We never shed a tear during a sappy movie before, yet here we are sobbing about someone returning home to their family in a coffee commercial.

But, strangely, along with this heightened emotionality, we may also feel more flexible and able to detach from what no longer serves us. The progressed Moon in Pisces rejects stagnation and seeks to keep moving. We may be exploring our creative talents during this time and discovering how important music and art are to us. This is a powerful time to give back to our communities, as the progressed Moon in Pisces is all about helping others. Just remember that the world's problems are not ours alone to solve. The progressed Moon in Pisces also demands we examine issues around setting boundaries. Indeed, during this time, we will learn major lessons about how we are all interconnected.

Glossary

AIR: One of the four elements, Air signs include Gemini, Libra, and Aquarius. Air signs are logical and social; they rarely leave home without a book or a buddy by their side.

CARDINAL: Cardinal signs are the first signs of each season: Aries, Cancer, Libra, and Capricorn. They are groundbreakers and trendsetters; they feel comfortable being in charge.

EARTH: One of the four elements, Earth signs include Taurus, Virgo, and Capricorn. Earth signs are physical and rational; they feel comforted by material security.

FIRE: One of the four elements, Fire signs include Aries, Leo, and Sagittarius. Fire signs are passionate and inspired; they always find a victory to celebrate.

FIXED: Fixed signs are the middle signs of each season: Taurus, Leo, Scorpio, and Aquarius. Fixed signs are creative and enduring; they have their own particular way they like things done.

HOUSE: Your birth chart contains twelve sectors, each representing a different area of life, like relationships or money.

MUTABLE: Mutable signs are the last signs of each season: Gemini, Virgo, Sagittarius, and Pisces. Mutable signs are flexible and all about communication; they always have the info, whether by intuitive measures or scientific abstracts.

WATER: One of the four elements, Water signs include Cancer, Scorpio, and Pisces. Water signs are emotional and intuitive; they feel most at home wherever there is music or art, as creative expression soothes them.

Acknowledgments

Thank you so much, Randon Rosenbohm and Sara David: Without your support, I would not have been able to write this book! Also, genius Callie Beusman, who taught me more about writing than anyone. A big thank-you to Andrew Luecke, Julie Popescu, Juhi Baig, and Sophie Saint Thomas, and to my family, for your daily love and encouragement! And thank you to my team at Chronicle for creating this book with me.